T0072334

Apokalypteria

Unveiling

the

Christ

of

Presence

PHILIP KRILL

AuthorHouse™
1663 Liberty Drive
Bloomington, IN 47403
www.authorhouse.com
Phone: 833-262-8899

Published by AuthorHouse 05/12/2023

ISBN: 979-8-8230-0799-3 (sc)
ISBN: 979-8-8230-0798-6 (e)

For

My Parents
Don (1949-2003) & Irma (1926-2013)

Divinely Present, then and now
Thank you

Introduction

This is the last in a trilogy of aphoristic reflections on the mystery of Presence.[1] Unlike my previous two books on this subject, *Apokalypteria* seeks to bridge the gap between those who are drawn to the mystery of Presence but have no hard and fast religious beliefs, and those devout and religious believers who view 'Presence' as a poor substitute when speaking about things sacred, holy and divine.

We are currently witnessing the great deconstruction of institutionalized Christianity.[2] This is as fortunate as it is inevitable. Christianity, as genuine, kerygmatic Evangel, defies definition. The proclamation of Christ dead, risen, ascended is uncontainable in any creed, dogma, social system or religious institution. Christianity is the dissolution of every form of status quo, giving rise to a communion of persons who know themselves to be in the world but not of the world for the life of the world.

This book is a babbling collection of effusive aphorisms spoken in an eschatological key which, despite (or perhaps because of) its repetitive and excessively redundant form, seeks to give witness to the Presence of Christ in the Mystery of Presence. *Apokalypteria* is offered in the hope that atheists, agnostics and believers alike may perceive their essential unity in the Mystery of Christ who is present in the Mystery of Presence. In the end, it is all a single Mystery - the triune Mystery of God.

Easter 2023

---

[1] *12 Wicker Baskets: Collected Fragments on the Mystery of Presence* and *Parousia: More Epiphanies on the Mystery of Presence.*
[2] See Bradley Jersek, *Out of the Embers: Faith After the Great Deconstruction.*

Presence is a participation in the Life of the Trinity. In Presence, we experience a self-transcendence that is of a piece with that of Father, Son, and Holy Spirit.

Presence is abiding in the *ex nihilo* of God's pure, creative act. In Presence, our nothingness is filled with the divine Love from which 'all was made was made' (cf. Jn. 1:3).

The peace of God is experienced in Presence. Presence is the *Plērōma*[3] of God's trinitarian Love peeking through the veil of Presence.

The experience of God is always more immediate than we comprehend or can express. God's glorious *Plērōma* reveals itself in Presence.

Presence is pregnant with the peace of God. Presence is the moment of never and forever in which the pre-eternal God communicates His infinite goodness.

Presence reveals freedom to be freedom from our need to deliberate. In Presence, there is nothing to decide since the truths we need are intuitively known.

---

[3] *Plērōma* (πλήρωμα) means 'fullness'. In Scripture it is used 17 times to indicate the fullness of God in Christ and of Christ in us (cf. Col. 2:9; Eph. 3:19), as well as the recapitulation and final glorification of all things in Christ.

Presence illumines the difference between discernment and deliberation. Discernment is of the spirit, deliberation of the mind.

In Presence, beginning and end, Alpha and Omega (cf. Rev. 2:13), are mystically united in an indefinable point of inseparable and unconfused union. Presence is the nowhere place where past and future fuse into a transcendental mystery of Now.

Actuality cannot be made into a noun. The experience of Presence saves us from reifying God.

The Mystery of Presence defies objectification. Like God, Presence can only be existentially apprehended, never conceptually captured or comprehended.

Presence is the condition for the possibility of thought, not its opposite. Presence is opposite of nothing but the Horizon of everything.

In Presence, nothing can be forced, nothing compelled. In Presence, all is given from a plērōmic Fullness, and only when the time is right.

In Presence, we experience a proleptic foretaste of the *Plērōma*. We blossom with a glorious peace that anticipates our final consummation in God.

Presence deconstructs the deconstructionists. Presence reveals that 'all have sinned and fall short of the glory of God' (cf. Rom. 3:23).

In Presence, we do not condemn, even those who condemn us (cf. Lk. 6:28, 37). Instead, Presence frees us from the spirit of condemnation and awakens us from its hypnotic spell.

Presence prevents us from judging even those who judge us harshly (cf. Mt. 7:1; 5:44). Presence makes us allergic to criticizing others.

Presence is not without wisdom, only without presumption. In Presence, we presume nothing yet understand everything.

Presence takes us beyond ideology and analytical thinking. In Presence, we seek understanding without indulging in foregone conclusions.

Presence is a space of divine gentleness in which the Wisdom of God is shared with us (cf. 1 Cor. 2:7). Abiding in Presence we can hear the 'small, still voice' of God (1 Kg. 19:12).

Presence reveals our lives as inherently purposeful, yet disabuses us of thinking we know what our final *telos* is. Presence allows us to know ourselves as persons blissfully 'known and hidden' in the inner Life of God (cf. Hos. 13:5; Jer. 1:5; Col. 3:3).

Our experience of Presence intimates the restoration of all things in God. *Apokatastasis*[4] seems the natural, inevitable *Plērōma* of abiding in Presence.

We cannot abide in Presence, and experience Presence as the transcendental meaning of being human, without also believing that 'all will be well, and all manner of things will be well'.[5]

Presence reveals the fabric of creation, right down to its unnecessary beginning, as permeated with the abiding love of God. In Presence, it is impossible not to be in divine bliss.

Our experience of Presence makes the notion of an eternal hell unimaginable. It reveals 'infernalist thinking' as a betrayal of human nature.[6]

---

[4] *Apokatastasis* means the restoration of the cosmos to a condition more beautiful and perfect that its original creation. It is also the *theologoumenon* that all human beings will eventually be saved. As widely contested in the current church as it was accepted in the early church, *Apokatastasis* remains the scandalous flashpoint for Christian theological speculation and comparative dogmatic studies.

[5] Julian of Norwich, *Revelations of Divine Love*.

[6] For a thorough analysis and dismantling of 'infernalist thinking' - both theological and philosophical - see David Bentley Hart, *That All Shall Be Saved: Heaven, Hell and Universal Salvation*.

Presence imparts an intuition of the goodness of being that is a sharing in heaven itself. Presence shows us that all the way to heaven is heaven, if only we have 'eyes to see and ears to hear' (cf. Dt. 29:4; Isa. 32:3; Mk. 8:18).

Presence knows not evil. Presence is an effulgence of God's Light 'in which there is no darkness' (cf. 1 Jn. 1:5). Those abiding in Presence cannot imagine the existence of evil.

Presence serves a governor on all that is said and written of it. Presence will censor any utterances about itself which do not exude bliss and joy (cf. Sir. 51:22).[7]

Presence is what inspires our mothers to say, 'If you don't have something nice to say about someone, say nothing at all'. Perhaps Jesus' mother told him the same thing: 'Let what you say be simply 'Yes' or 'No'; anything more than this comes from the Evil One' (cf. Mt. 5:37).

Presence mutes all but the praiseworthy tongue. 'Out of the fullness of the heart, the mouth speaks' (cf. Lk. 6:45). Nor should we speak unless, through Presence, we speak in love (cf. 1 Cor. 13).

---

[7] The book of *Sirach* is sometimes called the book of '*Ecclesiasticus*,' not to be confused with the book of *Ecclesiastes*.

Presence is what prevents 'winning the lotto' from becoming the purpose of our lives. In Presence, we enjoy life without looking to money or pleasure to supply its final meaning (cf. Mt. 6:20-24; 1 Tim. 6:10).

Presence keeps us from borrowing anyone's beliefs for our own (cf. Dt. 4:10; Ps. 119:33; Lk. 9:20). Presence allows us to existentially experience the promises of religion.

In Presence, we perceive everything as permeated with Light. Presence is a participation in the One who says, 'I am the light of the world' (cf. Jn. 9:5) and 'you are the light of the world' (cf. Mt. 5:14; cf. Eph. 5:8).

Presence is a created share in the uncreated Light of God. In Presence, we participate in a Presence greater than ourselves. In Presence, we are bathed in the light of God. In God's Light, 'we see light' (cf. Ps. 36:9).

Presence is an experience of being possessed by God in whose Embrace we become fully ourselves. Presence gives us a glimpse of knowing ourselves as we are known by God (cf. Jer. 1:5; Gal. 1:15).

In Presence, we experience ourselves as one with, yet completely other than, the Power that possesses us. In Presence, we grasp the truth that 'union differentiates, and perfect union differentiates perfectly'.[8]

---

[8] Phrase attributed, without specific reference in his writings, to Pierre Teilhard de Chardin: https://quoteinvestigator.com/2019/06/20/spiritual.

In Presence, we know ourselves like the Son knows Himself in the Father (cf. Jn. 10:30; 14:28; Gal. 2:20). Every moment in Presence, it's as if we hear the words that Jesus has heard from all eternity: 'This day I have begotten you' (cf. Ps. 2:7; Acts 13:33).

We experience Presence as Jesus experienced the Father - as a Power greater than us (cf. Jn. 10:30), yet as a Power who is also one with us (cf. Jn. 14:28).

The Holy Spirit is the Radiance of Presence that makes self-transcendence possible, both in us and in God. Every 'I-and-Thou' know each other as one in a Unity that is larger than, and identical with, their communion.

In Presence, we recognize 'otherness' as a divine excellence, not a created deficiency. In Presence, our sense of being 'other' from God is both affirmed and overcome (cf. Ps. 95:3; 1 Jn. 4:4).

'Otherness' as a divine excellence rather than a tragic deficiency stems from our life in the Trinity. In Presence, as in the Trinity, the 'Other' is beheld as 'My beloved' (cf. Song 5:10) not as a stranger (cf. Mt. 25:35).

Presence is a manifestation of the risen Christ, bringing us into a future *Plērōma* of His self-ascendent Love. In Presence, we 'rise with Christ are seated with, and in, Him at the right hand of God' (cf. Eph. 1:20; Col. 3:1).

Presence is the kenotic manifestation of God that envelops even (especially?) those who have no religion (cf. Lk. 19:10). Presence is the existential experience of the self-transcendent God to which all religion points.

Presence frees us from the need for religious argumentation or apologetics. In Presence, we realize the inherent - even demonic - fruitlessness of ideological debate (cf. Lk. 20:25).

Presence reveals evil to be the depraved practice of demonization (cf. Jn. 8:7). In Presence, we realize we cannot 'cast out Satan' by demonizing even the demonizers (cf. Mk. 3:23; Lk. 6:28).

Presence lifts us above ourselves. Presence never pits us against even those who poo-hoo the deifying power of Presence. In Presence, we have no adversaries - everyone is 'my mother, my brother, my sister' (cf. Mk. 3:35).

Living in Presence is living from the *Plērōma* in advance of the coming of God's kingdom. In Presence, God infuses our words and actions with the Light of His future glory (cf. 2 Cor. 3:13).

In Presence, the trinitarian self-presencing of God is ineffably communicated. In Presence, we feel ourselves caught up into a *perichoresis*[9] of Love which we recognize as our true, eternal home (cf. Jn. 14:23).

In Presence, we are both in and beyond ourselves in the same way God is both in and beyond creation. Presence is the sophianic Wisdom of God that traverses the unbridgeable gap between Creator and creature (cf. Prv. 8:22-36), between our true and egoic selves.

In Presence, the insuperable *diastasis*[10] between creature and Creator is traversed in a way that glorifies both God and man. Because of the sophianic Spirit of Presence, our 'otherness' from God is a means of our union with God, not separation from him.

Presence - the sophianic Spirit of God - makes self-possession possible both for God and for us. Just as Father and Son behold each other in the mirror of their Spirit, we see and take hold of ourselves in the light of that same Holy Spirit of Presence.

---

[9] *Perichoresis* (from Greek: περιχώρησις perikhōrēsis, 'rotation') is a term referring to the relationship of the three persons of the triune God (Father, Son, and Holy Spirit) to one another. *Circumincession* is a Latin-derived term for the same concept.
[10] *Diastasis* means 'distance' or 'separation'. In trinitarian theology, *diastasis* refers to the internal divine 'distance' between Father and Son. In its 'economic form' - i.e., the external manifestation of trinitarian relations in the historical Jesus - 'what seems to us to be the sign of separation of Father and Son is precisely the sign of greatest unification....'. Hans Urs von Balthasar, *Theo-Drama: Theological Dramatic Theory: The Last Act, volume 5*, p. 262.

In Presence, we transcend ourselves without leaving ourselves. Our experience of Presence reflects the way in which the Father and Son are eternally united but forever unconfused.

Presence reveals all forms of criticism as tacit aspirations for *plērōmic* Goodness (cf. Ps. 22). Presence is a participative share in God's *Plērōma* (1 Cor, 15:28) before its eschatological materialization.

Presence is the all-consuming Fire of God's transfiguring *Plērōma*, albeit in a state of latency. Presence is an 'already-but-not-yet' participation in God's final restoration of all things in Himself (Cf. Col. 1:20).

Presence is an existential, interior hieroglyph of a cosmic Pentecost (cf. Acts 2:1ff.) In Presence, we experience the *Shekinah*[11] of God as a future fullness (*Plērōma*) tacitly appearing in every present moment.

Presence is the '*Christification*' even of those who do not know Christ. In Presence, we experience ourselves 'in Christ,'[12] anointed with the same Spirit that alighted and rested upon Jesus, Son of Man, Son of God (cf. Mk. 1:10).

---

[11] *Shekhinah* (Hebrew: ùÀÑëÄéðÈä) is the English transliteration of a Hebrew word meaning 'dwelling' or 'settling' and denotes the *presence of God*, as it were, in a specific place. The prophets made numerous references to visions of the presence of God, particularly in the context of the Tabernacle or Temple, with figures such as thrones or robes filling the Sanctuary (cf. Isa. 6;1; Jer. 14:21; Ezek. 8:4).

[12] A phrase used by St. Paul over 164 times in epistles bearing his name. See the brilliant recapitulation of Pauline mysticism, particular regarding St. Paul's 'doctrine of participation,' in James D. G. Dunn, *The Theology of Paul the Apostle*. Grand Rapids, MI: William B. Eerdmans Publishing Co., 2006, pp. 390-410.

In Presence, our human nature, without substantial change, partakes of a divine glory that belongs to God alone (cf. 2 Pt. 1:4). Presence suffuses our humanity with iridescent trinitarian Light.

In Presence, we are assumed into God's trinitarian self-presencing, but without a fundamental change in our finite nature as creatures. In Presence, we become God in the same measure God became man in Christ.[13]

Presence gives us an existential share in the Paschal Mystery of Christ. In Presence, our false self is crucified and our true self, hidden with Christ in God (Col. 3:3), rises.

In Presence, death and resurrection are revealed as a single, simultaneous Mystery. The moment we stop thinking and simply become present, our ego vanishes and a kind of *plērōmic* love arises.

In Presence, the same Light that transfigured Christ on Mt. Tabor (cf. Mk. 9:2-8) transfigures us. Entering Presence is our equivalent of Jesus entering the Cloud of God's Presence on the mountain (cf. Ex. 24:15).

---

[13] Known as the doctrine of deification or divinization, this notion was the cornerstone of patristic theology. As St. Athanasius said, speaking for the entire patristic tradition, 'God became man so man could become God'. *On the Incarnation*, 54.

In Presence, we become radiant with the uncreated Light of God. In Presence, we become 'gods in God'.[14]

In Presence, the whole of humanity is present in the person towards whom we are present. In Presence, we are 'turned toward' the other in the same, divine way the Son is turned towards the Father (πρὸς τὸν θεόν) in their trinitarian Embrace (cf. Jn. 1:1-2).[15]

The Holy Spirit is the elusive *Pneumbra* of Love proceeding eternally from the self-presencing of Father and Son. In Presence, we are enveloped by this same edifying and deifying Spirit.

In Presence, like Christ, we cannot not look behold the 'other' without love (cf. Mk. 10:21). Presence creates a communion with the 'other' that dissolves the differences between us.

Presence is the source and substance of reconciliation. Presence is the sophianic Power of God's Spirit that 'draws all things' to God (cf. Jn. 12:31) and 'reconciles all things' in Him (cf. Col. 1:16-20).

Presence is a space of infinite compassion. In Presence, we are transported from the world of fault-finding into God's world of redemptive love.

---

[14] Another favorite patristic summation of the doctrine of deification. See above, n. 12.

[15] In Greek: πρὸς τὸν θεόν.

Presence shows the futility of 'kicking against the goad' (cf. Acts 26:14). In Presence, our complaints and sorrows, criticisms and fears are drowned in an ocean of divine mercy.

Presence illumines our lives with a supernal light that is as wise as it is beneficent. Presence is the Light of God in whose 'light we see light' (cf. Ps. 36:9).

In Presence, we experience ourselves as ever-greater than anything which we can imagine ourselves as. This reminds us of our essential union with God,[16] who is 'That of which nothing greater can be conceived'.[17]

Presence is always an experience of self-transcendence. It reminds us of Chesterton's quip: 'Angels can fly because they take themselves lightly'.[18]

---

[16] St. John of the Cross distinguishes between a 'substantial union' with God and a 'transformative' union of likeness' with Him. To wit: 'God sustains every soul and dwells in it substantially even though it may be the greatest sinner in the world. This union between God and creatures always exists. By it He conserves their being so that if the union should end, they would immediately be annihilated and cease to exist. Consequently, in discussing union with God we are not discussing the substantial union that always exists, but the soul's union with and transformation in God that does not always exist, except when there is likeness of love. We will call it the transformative union of likeness; and the former, the essential or substantial union'. *Ascent to Mt. Carmel, II, 5. 3.*

[17] St. Anselm, *Proslogium.*

[18] G.K. Chesterton, *Orthodoxy.*

Presence delivers us from demonization and imparts to us an angelic spirit. We realize our mission, like that of the angels, is to guide others into the beatitude of Presence (cf. Ps. 91:11).

In Presence, God sanctifies the world with every step we take. As our feet kiss the ground, it's as if God says again, 'Let there be light!' (Gen. 1:3).

Presence is an experience of 'I am there for you,' and 'You have my undivided attention'. In Presence, we intuit the *perichoretic* Presence of Father, Son and Spirit.

In Presence, we reconnect with our virginal innocence. In Presence, we catch a glimpse of ourselves as we are known by God 'before the foundation of the world' (cf. Eph. 1:4).

Christ's admonitions, 'Stay awake!' (cf. Mt. 24:42) could be translated as, 'Stay present to the present moment!' We will never be closer to God than we are now because it is never not Now.

In Presence, we open to the other, revealing the face we had before we were born. In Presence, we have an intimation of who we are in God 'before we were conceived in our mother's womb' (cf Jer. 1:5; Job 31:15).

Presence enhances our appreciation of particularity. In Presence, we give ourselves entirely to the one we are with. Presence is of a piece with the Incarnation, in which God gives Himself entirely to us in the particular person of His Son, *Emmanuel* (cf. Mt. 1:23).

Presence perceives the blessedness of everything in creation. In Presence, we participate in the joy of God when, beholding all God has made, he pronounced, 'It is good, very good!' (cf. Gen. 1:31).

God is beyond forgiveness, since, with the Father, Son and Spirit what is there to forgive? Similarly with Presence. In Presence, there is nothing to forgive since Presence is an immediate release from resentments that require forgiveness.

Presence is patient with imperfection. Patience is a participation in God's everlasting love, especially for the imperfect (cf. Mt. 9:13; Lk. 19:10).

God's reasons for loving us infinitely is God Himself, for 'God is love' (1 Jn. 4:8). Those who abide in Presence - which is the innermost essence of love - abide in God (1 Jn. 4:16).

God's is a why-less love. God loves because God is love (1 Jn. 4:8). God does what God is. So also in Presence. Presence is an 'I am here for you' without reason or explanation.

In Presence, we hold the other like a vet cradles a wounded bird. In Presence, we experience and exhibit the Presence of God for whom 'even the sparrows' are infinitely beloved (cf. Lk. 12:4-7).

The divine Mystery of Presence reveals itself in reflexive pronouns. After all, who is speaking when we say, 'I caught myself,' or 'I'm not myself today'? Is it not the One who also says, 'I am who I am' (Ex. 3:14)?

In Presence, we take everything with a grain of salt. In so doing we serve as 'the salt of the earth' (cf. Mt. 5:13) which preserves and freshens everything it touches.

Presence delivers us from the suffering that comes from resisting reality as it is in the present moment. In Presence, we discover the truth of Jesus' words, 'resist not evil, but overcome evil with love' (cf. Mt. 5:39; Rom. 12:21).

In Presence, we realize that 'acceptance is the answer to all our problems today'.[19] In Presence, we identify with Mary who said, 'Let it be to me as God desires' (cf. Lk. 1:38) and with her Son who said, 'Not my will, O God but Yours be done' (cf. Mt. 26:39).

---

[19] A phrase borrowed from *Alcoholics Anonymous*.

Presence is the power of perfect relinquishment. In Presence, we enter the Redeemer's final act of surrender: 'Father, into your hands I commit my spirit' (cf. Lk. 23:46; cf. Ps. 31:5).

Presence gives us the ability to disagree agreeably. It's only by abiding in Presence that we can 'make an effort to settle matters with our accusers' lest we imprison ourselves in resentment and are 'not released until we have paid the last penny' (cf. Lk. 12:58–59).

In Presence, 'we intuitively know how to handle situations that used to baffle us'.[20] In Presence, we partake of the Wisdom (Sophia) which discerns everything, including 'the secrets of the heart' (Ps. 44:21) and 'even the deep things of God' (cf. 1 Cor. 2:10).

Presence dissolves our problems. In Presence, we discover the meaning of Christ's words, 'Seek first the kingdom of God and all these other things will be given you as well' (cf. Mt. 6:33; Lk. 12:31).

Those who practice Presence may still practice religion, but they do so as an extension, not an evasion, of the power of Presence. In Presence, we realize that 'the Sabbath was made for man, not man for the Sabbath' (cf. Mk. 2:27).

---

[20] Quote taken from the 'Promises' of Alcoholics Anonymous. See the book, *Alcoholics Anonymous*, pp. 83-84

The power and permanence of Presence is the taproot of religion. In Presence, we 'go to our inner room, close the door, and pray to our Father in secret, and the Father who sees in secret repays us' (cf. Mt. 6:6).

When being present becomes our default mode, we experience the bliss of deification (*theosis*). 'Saints' are those who practice Presence as their permanent *modus operandi*.

Presence is a mystery of letting-go-ness (*Gelassenheit*).[21] In Presence, we enter into the self-emptying of Christ who 'did not deem equality with God a thing to be grasped at but relinquished Himself completely, assuming the form of a servant' (cf. Php. 2:6-11).

In Presence, self-emptying brings self-fulfillment, and surrender is experienced as triumph. In Presence, our *kenosis* (self-divestment) is our *theosis* (divinization).

Presence is of an altogether different order from the dualities and polarities of the world. In Presence, we learn the meaning of God's words, 'My ways are not your ways, my thoughts not your thoughts' (Isa. 55:8).

---

[21] *Gelassenheit* is an untranslatable German word that can be rendered 'letting-be-ness'. For year of meditations on the power of *Gelassenheit*, see my book, *Gelassenheit: Day-by-Day with Meister Eckhart*.

Presence brings divine bliss to those who enter it. In Presence, we fulfill Jesus' desire 'that my joy may be in you and your joy be complete' (cf. Jn. 15:11; 17:13).

In Presence, our awareness of the goodness of creation brings peace, joy, and bliss: *Sat* (Being), *Chit* (Awareness), *Bliss* (Ananda) - *Sacchidānanda*.[22] In Presence, we have already passed from death to life' (cf. Jn. 5:24).

Worry consumes those unfamiliar with Presence. In Presence, we imitate the flowers of the field who 'neither work nor spin yet are clothed by God more gloriously than Solomon in all his splendor' (cf. Mt. 6:28–29).

Presence is the epiphany of divine love in a finite world. In Presence, the Spirit of God overflows us like glowing lava from a volcano.

One person practicing Presence releases more of God's peace into the world than all the world's do-gooders (cf. Lk. 10:41-42).

One moment of Presence brings more joy than a lifetime of pleasure. After all, 'what does it profit a person to gain the whole world and lose a transcendent sense of self in the process' (cf. Mk. 8:36)?

---

[22] *Sacchidānanda is* a Hindu term that connotes the divine Bliss (*Ananda*) that arises within us when our Awareness (*Chit*) rests in Being (*Sat*), not in thinking.

In Presence, 'one day is as a thousand years, and a thousand years as one day' (2 Pt. 3:8). 'Better one day in the courts of Presence than a thousand elsewhere' (Ps. 84:11).

In Presence, even death appears as a manifestation of divine life and love. In Presence, we partake of the death and resurrection of Christ as a seamless, existential Mystery.

In Presence, there are no problems, just as in God 'there is no darkness' (1 Jn. 1:5). Presence banishes our problems, just as God's light banishes the darkness (cf. Jn. 1:5).

All that bedevils us dissolves when Presence arises. Presence is the risen Christ telling the demons 'Be gone!' (cf. Mk. 1:25).

Like Dracula fleeing the rising sun, that which troubles us flees before the light of Presence. In Presence, God's 'perfect love drives out all fear' (1 Jn. 4:18).

Presence is possessed of no possessiveness. In Presence, we 'take no provisions for the journey' (cf. Mk. 6:8) yet receive 'overabundant blessings in this present age and eternal life in the age to come' (cf. Lk. 18:30).

Presence, like the word, 'God,' presents as a noun, but is neither subject nor object. God is the 'Mystery of Presence' that makes our awareness of subjects and objects possible (cf Ps. 36:9; Jn. 1:9).

We experience the power of Presence when we become aware of our own awareness. This 'awareness of our awareness' is a participation in the self-presencing of God - Father, Son, and Holy Spirit (cf. 1 Cor. 2:10).

Presence is a transcendental mystery known when we become conscious of consciousness itself. In Presence, we know ourselves as the Father knows Himself in the Son (cf. Mt. 11:27), and we understand how the Son can say, 'When you have seen me, you have seen the Father' (cf. Jn. 14:9).

Presence is a state of unprejudiced openness - an intentional, attentive emptiness in which intimacy and revelation occur. This is the desert wilderness where God leads us and 'speaks tenderly to our hearts' (cf. Hos. 2:16).

Speaking - as opposed to Listening - is fraught with danger. Often it is nothing other than verbal mind-streams colliding with each other. In Presence, we understand why Jesus says, 'Let your 'Yes' mean 'Yes,' and your 'No' mean 'No'. Anything more is from the evil one' (cf. Mt. 5:37).

Thinking proliferates like wildfire. *Gaps in our thinking* is where Presence makes itself fit. In Presence, we say to the mind, 'Be still and know that God is God' (cf. Ps. 46:10).

Judgments and interpretations eliminate our capacity to be present. In Presence, we experience God saying to us, 'Judge not lest you be judged' (cf. Mt. 7:1).

The world of the ego (sin) is a delusional system governed by blame and shame. In Presence, we hear the voice of God, 'Has no one condemned you? Neither do I condemn you; go, and sin no more' (cf. Jn. 8:10–11).

Entering Presence is possible in every life situation, even those we label as tragic or unbearable. In Presence, we realize that 'even if I lie flat in *Sheol* (hell), You are there' (Ps. 139:8).

Near death experiences (NDE) confirm that death itself is a prime opportunity to experience Presence. In Presence, we share the awakening of Job: 'Slay me though he might, I will wait for him…for I know that my vindicator lives, and that he will at last stand forth upon the dust' (Job 13:15, 19:25).

Presence drives out all fear, even the fear of death (cf. 1 Jn. 4:18).

Drama is the opposite of Presence. Huffing and puffing find no place in Presence. God is not found in the emotional earthquake, firestorm or gale, but 'in the small, still voice' (cf. 1 Kg. 19:22).

Ego creates anxiety when we identify with the stories we tell ourselves about ourselves. In Presence, we discover that our true identity is 'hidden with Christ in God' (Col. 3:3).

Looking for our purpose in the past or the future is futile. We are known by God 'before the foundation of the world' (cf. Eph. 1:4). In Presence, we discover our life's purpose through a participation in His Eternal Now.

Our purpose in life is discovered by being totally present to the present moment. When, in Presence, we forget ourselves, we 'find ourselves' (cf. Mt. 16:25).

We will never be closer to God than we are now because it is never not now. In Presence, we realize that 'even before a word is on our tongues, O Lord, you know it' (Ps. 139:4).

Non-resistance to the present moment is the portal to Peace. In Presence, we hear God say, 'Offer no resistance to one who is evil but overcome evil with good' (cf. Mt. 5:39; Rom. 12:21).

Ego feasts on over-thinking. Presence fasts from mental indulgence. In Presence, we *listen* to God as did Mary of Bethany at the feet of Jesus (cf. Jn. 11:2). In Presence, we hear God saying, 'Blessed are the eyes that see what you see, the ears that hear what you hear' (cf. Mt 13:16).

Spiritual people do not mistake spiritual *ideas* for the experience of Presence. In Presence, we realize that 'God prays within us with sighs too deep for words' (cf. Rom. 8:26).

If we are *thinking* about God, the immediacy of God eludes us. 'Eye has not seen, nor ear heard, nor the human heart conceived, what God has prepared for those' who seek Him in Presence. (cf. 1 Cor. 2:9).

Presence is an attentive awareness, a virginal openness, an unimpeded receptivity. In Presence, we conceive of God as did Mary when she said, 'Let it be done to me according to Your desire' (cf. Lk. 1:38).

Presence is a spacious allowing, a total surrender, an unconditional acceptance, affirming all who enter it. Presence is our participation in the One who says, 'Come to me and I will give your rest' (cf. Mt. 11:28).

It is not the suffering with which He died, nor the blood which He shed, that constitutes the power of Christ's redemptive death. Instead, it is the Presence with which He accomplished it. Only in Presence is it possible to say, 'Father, forgive them' (cf. Jn. 23:34) and 'Into Your hands I commend my spirit' (cf. Lk. 23:46).

By dying Christ destroyed our death, by rising restored our life. This he achieved by assimilating our suffering and death into his deathless Presence with the Father (cf. Jn. 8:29).

Presence reveals 'death' as the inner dynamic of God's own triune Life. In Presence, we 'die to ourselves' in a manner analogous to the way the Father 'dies to Himself' in begetting the Son, and the Son 'dies to Himself' in allowing Himself to be begotten by the Father.[23] The Holy Spirit, in His self-effacing invisibility, facilitates and reveals the inherently kenotic Life of both the Trinity and of ourselves.

In Presence, 'we are already seated with Christ at the right hand of God' (cf. Eph. 2:6). The Father's 'right hand' is his Son, who himself is the self-presencing of the Father. When we abide in Presence, therefore, we 'abide in God' (cf. 1 Jn. 4:15).

---

[23] As Hans Urs von Balthasar says: 'The Son even cooperates in his begetting by letting himself be begotten, by holding himself in readiness to be begotten...'The Son prefers nothing to doing the Father's will, for even in being begotten he carries it out...On the other hand the Father also gives him the distance inherent in his independence...The divine processions occur in eternal simultaneity,' so that the Father's very act of begetting 'is an act of surrender to the Son, to which the Son replies with his surrender'.' *Theo-Drama: Theological Dramatic Theory, V: The Last Act,* p. 87, citing Adrienne von Speyr, *The World of Prayer,* p. 213.

Our *'fall from grace'* is forgetfulness of Presence. When we 'fall' from Presence, we are cast out into thinking - a kind of 'outer darkness' (cf. Mt. 25:30) in which there is heard the 'wailing and gnashing of teeth' (cf. Mt. 8:12).

Suffering continues for as long as it takes for us, like the prodigal son, 'come to our senses' and return to the redemptive power of Presence. Practicing Presence is always a 'return to the home of our Father' (cf. Lk. 15:17-18).

Presence is a raid on the Unspeakable. In Presence, like 'great high priests,' we enter the Holy of Holies (cf. Heb. 9:3) where God abides in an emptiness filled with silent music.

In Presence, our personal uniqueness is not dissolved but enhanced. In Presence, God gives to us a mystical 'white stone with a new name written on it which no one knows except the one who receives it'. (cf. Rev. 2:17).

In Presence, we 'lose our lives' only to 'find them' (cf. Mt. 16:25). Presence is the dissolution of the ego and the liberation of our true self known only by God (cf. Col. 3:3). In Presence, we 'are set free with the freedom of the children of God' (cf. Rom. 8:21).

We are not the voices in our heads. We are not the labels we apply to ourselves. We are those who 'lives are hidden with Christ in God' (Col. 3:3) and who discover their true identities in Presence.

We are always greater than that which we label ourselves. Our 'we-are-ness' always precedes the fact that we are this or that. Before we are this or that, we *are*. We are they who are *in* the One who is I AM (cf. Ex. 3:14-15).

The Mystery of Presence is the experience of being present, enveloped and sustained by a Power *greater than* ourselves. Persons who are present to themselves and to others co-inhere with the infinite Presence of God that makes personal presence possible (cf. 1 Cor. 13:12).

God is the ineffable and eternally prior Mystery of Presence from which our capacity to be present comes (cf. 1 Jn. 4:19). The supra-essential Presence we call 'God' precedes and makes possible our experience of self-transcendence.

Who we *think* we are is never who we *really* are. In Presence, we realize that we are *not* what we think we are. Outside of Presence, it's as if we hear God saying, 'I do not know you' (cf. Lk. 13:25).

Forgetfulness of Presence is the origin of fear, doubt and insecurity. Presence is the death of ego and the birth of the spirit (cf. Rom. 8:5).

Presence is the mystical Calvary. Presence crucifies the ego so we can rise from the dead in Presence.

Presence is the 'sacrifice acceptable to the Lord,' i.e., 'a humble, contrite heart' (cf. Isa. 57:15; Ps. 51:17). Presence is a manifestation of the Divine Mercy in which everything is redeemed (cf. Rom. 11:32).

Presence is the fulfillment of Christ's command, 'Go and learn the meaning of the words, 'I desire mercy, not sacrifice'' (cf. Mt. 9:13; cf. Hos. 6:6). In Presence, saints and sinners alike find an unconditional acceptance that makes all such distinctions irrelevant (cf. Mt. 5:45).

In Presence, the Spirit of God flows down upon us like fine oil on the head, running down upon the beard, upon the beard of Aaron, upon the collar of his robe' (Ps. 133:2). Presence 'christifies' us with same Spirit that alighted upon Jesus (cf. Jn. 1:32) who, for this reason, is called 'the Christ,' i.e., the Anointed One.

Dis-identification with personal descriptives is the first step to personal discovery. This is why Jesus insists 'only those who lose their lives' - i.e., disidentify with egoic self-concepts - 'will find them' (cf. Mt. 16:25).

Ego is inherently self-destructive. In the end, 'Satan casts out Satan' (cf. Mt. 12:26), as the suffering we endure because of our sins becomes the cause of our salvation when we 'let go and let God'.

In Presence, our sinful selves disappear, but we do not (cf. Rom. 8:6). In Presence, 'if someone's work is burned up, that one will suffer loss, yet the person will be saved, albeit as through fire' (cf. 1 Cor. 3:15).

Everyone experiences pain but suffering is always optional. Suffering comes from telling ourselves dreadful stories about our pain. In Presence, we don't 'worry about tomorrow,' knowing 'tomorrow will take care of itself' and that 'sufficient for each day is its own evil' (cf. Mt. 6:34).

Presence is the unfailing solvent for our self-centered actions. Our inner demons flee when we practice Presence, shouting as they go, 'we know who you are - the Holy One of God' (cf. Lk. 4:34).

To abide in Presence is to find 'space'. To find space is to find relief. In Presence, it's as if we hear the Lord say, 'Let her alone. Why do you make trouble for her? She has done a good thing for me' (cf. Mark 14:6)

Paradise is living in a state of continuous Presence. In Presence, we have 'already passed from death to life' (cf. Jn. 5:24).

The fires of hell singe our souls whenever we depart from Presence. 'Better to enter into the kingdom of God (Presence) with one eye than with two eyes to be thrown into the fires of Gehenna' (cf. Mk. 9:47).

Presence is the Space of *No-thought (Mushin)*,[24] but *No-thought* does not mean no awareness. In Presence, we become as 'thoughtless' as children but sagacious as serpents (cf. Mt. 10:16).

Presence is a state of relaxed receptivity, of childlike wonderment. In Presence, we become 'as little children, fit for the kingdom of God' (cf. Mt. 18:3).

Awareness precedes explanation and appreciation precedes analysis. Presence is a participation in God's prevenient appreciation of all He has made (cf. Gen. 1:31).

In Presence, we behold the lilies of the field and the birds of the air as sacraments of God's love (cf. Mt. 6:28). Presence is a participation in the primordial Love of our Creator.

Being present is always prior to, and more powerful than, being right or wrong. In Presence, we hear the words of God, 'Neither do I condemn you; go, and sin no more' (cf. Jn. 8:11).

In Presence, we have no desire to argue with God or with each other. In Presence, we never 'approach the Lord in order to test Him' (cf. Mk. 10:2).

---

[24] See my book, *Mushin: Meditations on the Mystery of Mindfulness.*

Presence is Spirit-intoxication. Presence inebriates us with 'the new wine' of God's kingdom (cf. Lk. 5:38; Mk. 14:25).

In Presence, we *look at* our impatience from a place *beyond* impatience. In Presence, we *notice* our anger from a place that is *immune* to anger. This place is called 'the kingdom of God' (cf. Mk. 1:15).

Are Presence and God identical? Not exactly. God is glimpsed in the experience of Presence, but God is always the infinite, indefinable *Horizon* in which the experience of Presence takes place.

God is the indefinable *Background* to every possible foreground. God is the world's *Negative Space*.

Presence is acceptance and acceptance is peace. In Presence, we experience the 'peace that passes all understanding' (cf. Php. 4:7)

We are never who we *think* we are. We are always only those who are able to *observe* they think they are something other than 'they are'. Our 'lives are hidden with Christ in God' (Col. 3:3).

As the power of Presence grows stronger within us, we no longer have ears for the voices in our heads. In Presence, we are delivered from our mental 'tower of Babel' (cf. Gen. 11:7), attuned only to the quiet words of God spoken in our hearts (cf. Hos. 2:14; 1 Kg. 19:12).

Presence in us always speaks to the power of Presence in the other. *Cor ad cor loquitur:* heart speaks to heart.[25] Between such hearts flow 'rivers of living water...welling up unto eternal life' (cf. Jn. 4:14; 7:38).

Histrionics are the stuff of our sinful selves, but also opportunities to return to Presence. When we notice we have sinned - i.e., departed from Presence - it's as if our sins instantly dissolve in a sea of divine understanding (cf. Isa. 1:18; Lk. 7:47-48).

To understand completely is to forgive completely. Presence is the space of unconditional understanding and absolute forgiveness. Presence is the voice of God saying, 'Judge not lest you be judged' (cf. Mt. 7:1).

In Presence, we apprehend the miracle of being. In Presence, we hear the first words of God, 'Let there be light' (cf. Gen. 1:3).

Presence functions like a magnet for others. When we abide in Presence, others feel they could be healed simply by 'touching the fringe' of our garments (cf. Mt. 9:20).

---

[25] The motto of St. John Henry Cardinal Newman.

Presence is a mystery of spacious acceptance and serenity. In Presence, we hear the voice of the risen Christ, 'Peace be with you!' (cf. Jn. 20:21).

Beauty is the power of Presence manifesting itself in the world. 'How beautiful are the feet of those' who walk in the world of Presence (cf. Isa. 52:7; Rom. 10:15).

Beauty is arresting. Beauty stops us in our tracks and quickens our pulse. Beauty momentarily stops our thinking and opens us to Presence. In that opening, God 'enters in and takes up his home in our hearts' (cf. Jn. 14:23; Rev. 3:20).

Remaining in Presence is the way, not only to appreciate beauty, but to become beautiful. Presence beatifies us with the iridescent glory of God (cf. Ps. 21:5; 2 Cor. 3:18).

Presence is empty of thought but saturated with Power. Presence is the Power of the same divine Nothingness from which the Big Bang proceeded (cf. Gen. 1:1).

Presence is a place beyond thinking in which creative genius appears. Presence is the interior void in which creativity arises, just as creation itself emerged from the void *ex nihilo* (cf. Gen. 1:2).

Presence is the place of *No-mind*, yet it is also the place of super-essential alert awareness and receptivity. In Presence, 'it has been given to us to know the secrets of the kingdom of God' (cf. Mt. 13:11).

When we abide in Presence, we intuit 'what is the breadth and length and height and depth' of the love of God (cf. Eph. 3:18). Without Presence, 'we look but do not see, listen but neither hear nor understand' (cf. Mt. 13:13).

Presence is engagement without attachment, involvement without dependence. In Presence, we experience God's relationship with the world: wholly immanent (cf. Col. 1:16; Mt. 28:20) yet utterly transcendent (cf. Isa. 55:9).

Presence is the sophianic *penumbra* of eternity imparting to every temporal moment its depth and meaning. In Presence, we have 'already passed from death to life' (cf. Jn. 5:24; 1 Jn. 3:14).

Our experience of Presence belies the philosophy of *Advaita*.[26] In Presence, we lose our false selves (cf. Lk. 17:33), but discover our true identity in God (cf. Jer. 1:5).

---

[26] *Advaita* is the philosophy of physical and metaphysical non-duality.

Presence is the destruction of the ego, or false self, not the dissolution of the unique, unrepeatable, and unsubstitutable persons God created us to be. God knows us 'before we were conceived in our mother's womb' (cf. Job 31:15), predestining us 'before the foundation of the world to be holy and blameless in his sight' (cf. Eph. 1:4).

If Presence were the annihilation of the self, there would be no 'I' to notice or say such things. We 'are' because God 'is' (cf. Ex. 3:14).

Every pause in the mind-stream is an in-breaking of Presence. In the gaps between our thoughts, we discover the stillness in which the whispers of God's Spirit can be heard (cf. Ps. 46:10; Mt. 6:6).

Whenever there is a break in our thinking, 'the Kingdom of God is at hand' (cf. Mt. 3:2). For God's 'thoughts are not our thoughts, nor God's ways our ways' (cf. Isa. 55:8). 'Be still,' says the Lord, 'and know that I AM' (Ps. 46:10).

The ego flourishes in time but the spirit in Presence. In Presence, we are already 'seated with Christ at the right hand of the Father' (cf. Eph. 2:6; Col. 3:1).

In Presence, the sweetness of eternal life seems palpable. In Presence, it's as if we can 'taste and see the goodness of the Lord' (cf. Ps. 34:8).

Presence is where chastity and ecstasy kiss and where 'purity of heart' replaces possessiveness as our *modus operandi* (cf. Prv. 22:11; Ps. 73:1; Mt. 5:8). In Presence, our desires are deified and we receive the virginal fecundity befitting a bride of Christ (cf. Isa. 62:5; 2 Cor. 11:2).

In Presence, time stands still. In Presence, we understand that 'with the Lord one day is as a thousand years, and a thousand years as one day' (cf. 2 Pt. 3:8).

Presence is filled with wisdom, light and love. In Presence, 'our hearts are burning within us' as God 'explains everything to us' (cf. Lk. 24:32).

Hand-wringing evaporates when Presence replaces thinking as our default position. In Presence, we hear the voice of God: 'Do not be afraid, only have faith' (cf. Lk. 8:50).

Direct experience happens only in the present moment. In Presence, 'the kingdom of God draws near' (cf. Lk. 21:31) and 'is now here' (cf. Jn. 4:23; 5:25).

In Presence, we experience God as the Power of the Now. The Now is 'the fullness of time' (cf. Eph. 1:10; Gal. 4:4) in which the Light of God appears.

When the future arrives - if there were such a thing - it can only ever appear as another Now. Nothing real exists in the past or the future. Memories are but mental abstractions, often preventing us from seeing that, in Presence, God 'makes all things new' (cf. Rev. 21:5).

In Presence, we become, as it were, 'a new creation; the old has passed away, and the new has come' (cf. 2 Cor. 5:17).

Presence is unrestricted openness, unfiltered acceptance. In Presence, all resistance to what exists melts away in an ocean of understanding and forgiveness. In Presence, we hear Jesus' words: 'Go in peace, your faith has made you well' (cf. Lk. 17:19).

That which we resist persists. In Presence, demonizing ceases. In Presence, we realize that 'Satan cannot cast out Satan' (cf. Mk. 3:23), and every attempt to do so results in 'seven other spirits more evil entering us and our last state becoming worse than our first' (cf. Lk. 11:26).

Learning to be fully present to the present moment is the spiritual equivalent of splitting the atom. The release of creative energy is unimaginable. In Presence, we experience a perpetual Big Bang in which God says, 'Let there be light!' (cf. Gen. 1:3, 15).

Presence is alert attentiveness to the power of the present moment. In Presence, we experience the creative action of God, not as a past event, but as an ever-present miracle. In Presence, we know God as *Emmanuel*, i.e., God-with-us (cf. Mt. 1:23).

Presence is God loving God's-self in and through every person. Presence is the sophianic fulfillment of Jesus' prayer, 'that they may be one even as we are one, Father, I in them and you in me, that they may become perfectly one' (cf. Jn. 17:21–23).

Presence is a space of perfect joy. In Presence, the promise of Jesus comes true: 'that my joy may be in you, and that your joy may be full' (cf. Jn. 15:11).

Human thinking cannot solve the problems it creates. In Presence, we acquire divine wisdom and peace. In Presence, we learn to 'think as God does, not as human beings do' (cf. Mt. 16:13).

Wisdom comes from the 'intuition of being', discovered in Presence. Presence arises from a felt-sense of one' own *I-am-ness*. In Presence, we become aware of our unity with, yet otherness from, God who is 'I AM' (cf. Ex. 3:14). In Presence, we are both divinely illumined and humanly humbled.

Discovering Presence, we are in possession of 'the buried treasure' for which we are willing to 'give up everything' (cf. Mt. 13:44). Shifting our focus from thinking to Presence, we suddenly recognize the present moment as 'the time of our visitation' (cf. Wis. 3:7; Lk. 19:14).

Everyone has fleeting moments of Presence. Even those who identify completely with the voices in their heads have brief stoppages in their incessant mental activity. Learning how to *stretch* these moments of Presence into an abiding peace is 'the key to opening the kingdom of God' (cf. Mt. 16:19; Lk. 17:20).

Suicide can be understood as an attempt to disidentify with the voices in our heads and to discover the peace of Presence. We need only to 'die to ourselves' (cf. Rom. 14:7), not kill ourselves, to find the 'peace of God that surpasses all understanding' (cf. Php. 4:7).

The experience of hell is permitted by God in order to bring us to heaven. When the pain of holding on becomes greater than the pain of letting go, we let go.[27] In Presence, we share in the salvific letting-go of Christ: 'Father, into your hands I commit my spirit' (cf. Lk. 23:46; Ps. 31:5).

Immersed in the silence and stillness of Presence, we share in divine peace. Presence is the existential experience of Jesus' promise; 'Come to me, all you who are weary and heavy burdened, and I will give you rest' (cf. Mt. 11:28).

---

[27] Saying attributed to Alcoholics Anonymous.

Presence is an ever-new astonishment at the miracle of being. In Presence, we delight that 'we are wondrously made' and that all things manifest 'the glory of God' (cf. Ps. 139:14; 19:1).

Death is not the opposite of life, just as darkness is not the opposite of light. Life and Light, like God, have neither equal nor opposite. In Presence, we experience God 'as the God of the living, not of the dead' (cf. Lk. 20:38).

Presence is a mystery of light and life. In Presence, we experience the risen Christ 'in whom is life, and whose life is the light of the human race' (cf. Jn. 1:4).

Presence is a share in the uncreated light of God. In Presence, we realize that 'God is light and in him is no darkness at all' (cf. 1 Jn. 1:5).

Presence is utterly disarming. Presence divests us of pretense and gently unveils the divine Source of our existence. In the benevolent light of Presence, we experience 'the Way, the Truth, and the Life' (cf. Jn. 14:6).

In Presence, we cultivate an interior emptiness filled with alert attentiveness. In Presence, we hear the words: 'Stay awake! You know not the time of your visitation' (cf. Sir. 18:20; Lk. 19:44).

Presence shows death to be an illusion of the mind. Presence is 'the light of God that the darkness of death cannot overcome' (cf. Jn. 1:5).

Presence precedes and exceeds all that appears within it, including the experience of death. Once in touch with the prevenience of Presence - which is pure love - the fear of death dissolves (cf. 1 Jn. 4:18).

Presence is a form of living death. In Presence, we 'lay down our lives, that we may take them up again' (cf. Jn. 10:17). We 'die to the deeds of the flesh (ego)' in order to 'live according to the spirit' (cf. Rom. 8:13).

In Presence, 'being here' for the other means we have, at least momentarily, 'died' to ourselves. Being present to another is a life-giving form of *life in death*.

Presence is a place of perfect poise. In Presence, we stand before the evils of the world as one with Christ who stood perfectly poised, self-possessed and filled with compassion before Pilate who condemned him (cf. Mt. 27:14; Mk. 14:61).

In Presence, we echo to the demonic forces of deception, accusation, division and death itself what Christ said to Pilate: 'You have no power over me...' (cf. Jn. 19:11).

Poised in Presence, we are bereft of thinking, yet abounding with an alert, loving attention. In Presence, we are mystically armed with 'the two-edged sword' of divine wisdom, 'living and active, piercing to the division of soul and spirit, discerning the thoughts and intentions of the heart' (cf. Heb. 4:12).

In Presence, we have no expectations of others. In Presence, we recognize that expectations are premeditated resentments. Seeing the faults and failures of our neighbor, our only response is, 'Lord, have mercy on me, a sinner!' (cf. Lk. 18:13).

Presence is a place of acute listening. In Presence, we hear the critical sound of 'the cock's crow' (cf. Lk. 22:60), followed by the consoling whispers of the Holy Spirit (cf. Jn. 3:8).

Presence is a space of expectant waiting, of hope-filled anticipation. In Presence, we are 'wise virgins' eagerly awaiting the 'arrival of their divine bridegroom' (cf. Mt. 25:2ff.).

Presence is the power of allowing and beholding. In Presence, we stand before the world as God did on the final day of creation, declaring, 'It is all good, very good!' (cf. Gen. 1:31).

Presence is the joy of sitting still. In Presence, we discover that stillness speaks. In Presence, we experience the Spirit of God praying within us 'with sighs too deep for words' (cf. Rom. 8:26).

Presence is thoughtless awareness. Presence is consciousness beyond cognition. In Presence, we are, as it were, 'caught up to heaven, intuitively hearing things that cannot be told, which no one may utter' (cf. 2 Cor. 12:2–4).

Presence is awareness of the Absolute - a transcendental intuition of the ever-greater mystery of being. Presence is a created participation in the uncreated Mystery of God. In Presence, God descends to us so that we may ascend to God.

Presence is a participation in the Infinite, whereas intellection is limited to the contingent, the relative, the finite. In Presence, we 'know the love of God which surpasses knowledge'. In Presence, we are 'filled with all the fullness of God' (cf. Eph. 3:19).

Presence is the spiritual kiln of our deification. In Presence, we are fired with the heat and light of the Holy Spirit, perfected as 'the work of the divine Potter's hand' (cf. Isa. 64:8; Jer. 8:14). In Presence, we relax into a malleable state in which God fashions us into vessel of His divine glory.

Presence is a dynamic of ever-deeper letting go (*Gelassenheit*). Presence is a participation in the self-emptying (*kenosis*) of Christ (cf. Php. 2:6-11) and, more primordially, in the *Ur-kenosis* of the Father.[28] In Presence, we are assimilated into the *perichoresis* of the Trinity.

Presence is a participation in the creative, and recreative, action of God. In Presence, - i.e., in a movement of inner and utter self-dispossession - our voices become one with that of God who says at every moment, '*Let it be…*' (cf. Gen. 1:3).

God expropriates himself, first within his own trinitarian Life, then, as an overflow of God's uncontainable love, into creation. Abiding in Presence, and surrendering ourselves in self-donation, we are taken into, and divinized by, God's self-diffusive love.

Letting be and letting go are symbiotic. They make for that mystical space of ever-expanding allowing, welcoming, accepting and receiving. In Presence, we experience the risen Christ saying, 'Come to Me, all you who labor and are heavy burdened, and I will give you rest' (cf. Mt. 11:28).

---

[28] Hans Urs von Balthasar speaks of three 'cascading kenoses,' flowing, as it were, from the Original or Ur-kenosis beginning with the Father in the Trinity: '[A] first kenosis of the Father, expropriating himself by generating' the consubstantial Son. Almost automatically, this first kenosis expands to a kenosis involving the whole Trinity. For the Son could not be consubstantial with the Father except by self-expropriation; and their We, that is, the Spirit, must also be God if he is to be the 'personal seal of that self-expropriation that is identical in Father and Son…This primal kenosis makes possible all other kenotic movements of God into the world; they are simply its consequence'. *Theo-Dramatics, IV*, p. 331.

In Presence, we become as 'little children,' fit for the kingdom of God (cf. Mt. 18:3). In Presence, Christ 'suffers us, his little children, to come to him' (cf. Lk. 18:16) and to inherit the 'kingdom he has prepared for us' (cf. Mt. 25:34) since 'before the foundation of the world' (cf. 1 Pt. 1:20).

At the core of our *being,* there is a radical openness that is both our true identity *and* the Presence of God. Presence awakens us to this openness - which is our salvation - and results in immediate, irrevocable bliss.

At the moment of death, many people experience pure Presence for the first time. The advent of death dissolves the ego and unveils the truth. In a single instant of Presence, 'we know the truth, the truth that sets us free' (cf. Jn. 8:32).

As death approaches, an eternal pregnant pause arises in which we discover our transcendental selfhood. A lifetime of sin evaporates in this smallest sliver of Presence. In Presence, we hear the words of Christ, 'This day you are with me in Paradise' (cf. Lk. 23:43).

In Presence, death and life are shown to be a single, seamless mystery. Presence is the death of illusions, judgments and possessiveness and the resurrection of peace, understanding and bliss. Presence is the Paschal Mystery in miniature.

'God' is the ineffable Mystery of tri-personal self-Presence making our experience of Presence possible. God constitutes our human nature *as* Presence. Presence is God's 'image and likeness' within us (cf. Gen. 1:26). In Presence, we become living icons of God's pre-eternal glory (cf. Jn. 17:10).

Death is a reality only for the sinful self. In Presence, we experience death as an opportunity - perhaps our greatest opportunity - to enter the salvific *kenosis* of Christ (cf. Php. 2:5-11). In Presence, we are dispossessed of ourselves but in possession of, and possessed by, the self-dispossessing God.

The Presence of God can only be *experienced,* never understood or explained. No one can see the face of God - i.e., endure his full-on Presence - and live (cf. Ex. 33:20). Yet, in Presence, we do 'see' God. In Presence, we are one with the Son of God, the Eternal Word, who was with God in the beginning, facing God from the beginning, and one with God from all eternity (cf. Jn. 1:1).

The Presence of God - i.e, the Source of our capacity to be present - is tacitly experienced whenever we cultivate a sense of spaciousness within us. When we open to 'an other' in Presence, we are opening to Christ himself (cf. Mt. 25:45), thus entering his own 'spacious unity' with the Father (cf. Jn. 14:9).

Knowledge of God is always oblique, tacit, untoward. In Presence, the promise of Jesus is fulfilled: 'that those who do not see may see, and that those who see may become blind' (cf. Jn. 9:39).

Presence is spacious awareness without agenda. In Presence, we intuit the silent, creative love of God who acts *ex nihilo*, unconditioned by anything other than God's own self-presencing (cf. Jn. 1:3, 10; Col. 1:16-17).

Dis-identification with any and every thought about anything or anyone is the result of Presence and the path to salvation. Hence, Jesus forbade anyone to speak of him as the 'Messiah' (cf. Lk. 9:21).

Presence takes us beyond labeling. In Presence, we behold the primordial, uncategorical goodness of all that is. When we label things, we hear the voice of Christ, 'Get behind me, satan, you are thinking as human beings do, not as God does' (cf. Mt. 16:23).

Presence is the 'rich soil' in which the seeds of God's Presence are planted and which 'bears much fruit' (cf. Jn. 15:5).

Presence is the mystery of surrender and relinquishment. In Presence, our demons are expelled and Christ's will is fulfilled: 'Unbind him and let him go' (cf. Jn. 11:44).

In Presence, we transcend ourselves without losing ourselves. In Presence, we know that God and we are one, and that God is greater than us (cf. Jn. 10:30; 14:28).

In Presence, we realize that we are identical neither with the ideas we have about ourselves nor the stories we tell about ourselves. In Presence, we realize we 'are also children of Abraham' (cf. Gal. 3:14, 29), i.e. heirs of the promise that Presence portends.

In Presence, our trust in the gratuity of being is immediate and unconditional. In Presence, we do not obsess 'about what we are to wear or what we are to drink' but instead resemble 'the lilies of the field and the birds of the air' who are regaled 'more beautifully than Solomon in all his splendor' (cf. Lk. 12:22-31).

Entering Presence is like ascending the Mount of Beatitudes. In Presence, we are imbued with purity of heart and catch a glimpse of God (cf. Mt. 5:8).

Presence is an arena of perfect peace. In Presence, we are made peacemakers and know ourselves as children of God (cf. Mt. 5:9).

Presence is a place of 'salt and light'. In Presence, we are preserved in divine freshness and made incandescent with divine illumination. In Presence, we become 'the salt of the earth and the light of the world' (cf. Mt. 5:13-15).

Presence is a mystery of divine alchemy. In Presence, our grief is transmuted into acceptance (cf. Mt. 5:4) and our 'sorrows are turned to joy' (cf. Jn. 16:20).

In Presence, we intuit our transcendent, inseparable union with God. In Presence, we sense that we can say with the God-man (Jesus), 'Before Abraham was, I am' (cf. Jn. 8:58).

In Presence, we enter a perpetual Pentecost. Presence is the Spirit of God, descending as the fire of God's holy *Sophia* (Wisdom) and enveloping us in a cloud of divinizing light and life (cf. Acts 2:3; Ex. 34:34-35).

Presence is our share in the messianic identity of Christ. In Presence, we are anointed with the same Spirit that proceeds from the Father and rests eternally upon the Son (cf. Lk. 4:18; Isa. 61:1).

Presence reveals to us, in a participative way, the 'mysteries of the kingdom of God' (cf. Lk. 8:10). In Presence, we share in the 'mind of Christ' (cf. Php. 2:5; 1 Cor. 2:16).

In Presence, we behold the contingent, changeable, finite, corruptible things of creation as delightful, not as deficient. In Presence, we behold all that withers and dies as an image of the deathless, self-emptying life of the Trinity.

In the Trinity, the Father gives the Son everything except his paternity, without, however, holding anything back for himself. Presence loses nothing of itself when it arises within us; Presence is a gift of self-transcending, divinizing love (cf. Jn. 6:39).

The relationship between God and the cosmos is a 'circulation' included in the infinite circumincession[29] of the Trinity. Presence initiates us into the *perichoresis* of God and awakens us to the seamlessness of the universe in and with God.

The Trinity is the fontal Mystery of infinite surrender and self-renunciation, as well as of ineffable fulfillment and self-realization. In Presence, we experience an absolute preference of the Thou for the I, yet with a fulfillment of the 'I' which is a share in the co-inherent joy of the Father and the Son (cf. Jn. 17:13).

The Trinity is a Mystery in which three divine Persons realize themselves both in and through each other. In Presence, we likewise experience ourselves as self-transcendent, i.e., related to ourselves and others, yet enveloped by a 'Spirit' that makes this differentiated unity possible.

Presence brooks no artificiality. Presence benevolently excludes the clichéd, the platitudinous, the trite. Presence is the 'mountain of the Lord' upon which only the 'richest foods and finest wine' of the Spirit is served (cf. Isa. 2:2; 25:6).

Presence is a fullness (*Plērōma*) of divine freshness. Abiding in Presence, we know the meaning of 'a new heaven and a new earth' (cf. Rev. 21:1).

---

[29] *Circumincession* is the Latin derivative of *perichoresis.*

Presence is a place of ever-greater gratitude, i.e., a 'eucharistic' space. In Presence, we become one with Christ who, in his eternal gratitude to the Father as the Father's only-begotten and beloved Son (cf. Mt. 3:17), gives himself as food 'for the life of the world' (cf. Jn. 6:51).

Presence is a space of relinquishment in which our greatest joy is to possess nothing. In Presence, we are filled with the Holy Spirit who wants nothing for himself but desires simply to be the pure manifestation and communication of the love between Father and Son (cf. Jn. 14:26; 16:13–15).

Presence makes any task enjoyable. Bliss is no further away than our willingness to give what's immediately at hand our full attention. In Presence, our vision is deified, allowing us 'to see the world in a grain of sand'.[30]

We are illumined from within by the light of Presence. In Presence, we know ourselves as 'the light of the world that cannot be hidden but which gives light to all in the house' (cf. Mt. 5:14–15).

Presence 'gives light to our eyes' (Bar. 1:12). When we look at another with soft eyes, we show them the face of God (cf. Jn. 14:9).

---

[30] *To see a World in a Grain of Sand, And a Heaven in a Wild Flower, Hold Infinity in the palm of your hand...*' are the opening lines of William Blake's poem, *Auguries of Heaven.*

'The eye through which I see God is the same eye through which God sees me; my eye and God's eye are one eye, one seeing, one knowing, one love.[31] In Presence, we understand 'as we have been fully understood' (cf. 1 Cor. 13:12).

In Presence, we are awed by the uncanny gratuity of existence. In Presence, we are brought up short by the awareness that 'it is not that we have loved God but that God has loved us first' (cf. 1 Jn. 4:19).

Presence is empty of everything but openness to the Infinite. Presence is a posture of unrestricted awe. In Presence, we know we 'are wondrously made' and all of God's works 'fill us with wonder' (cf. Ps. 139:14).

Presence is without judgment, analysis or division. Presence is fullness of peace absent perturbation. When we enter Presence, the 'scarlet of our sins' turns instantly white (cf. Isa. 1:18).

In Presence, there is neither fear nor evil. In Presence, we experience the 'perfect love that 'casts out fear' (cf. 1 Jn. 4:18), and the divine power that 'expels all the demons' (cf. Mk. 1:34).

---

[31] Saying attributed, without reference, to Meister Eckhart. See: https://www.goodreads.com/quotes/7169-the-eye-through-which-i-see-god-is-the-same.

In Presence, the beauty of the Infinite is self-evident, inspiring immediate bliss. In Presence, 'even the darkness is not dark, and the night is bright as the day' (cf. Ps. 139:12).

Presence is where the actuality of existence is mystically apprehended. Presence is an intuition of being, a tacit grasp of the absolute fortuity of all that is. In Presence, we echo the words of the psalmist, 'Taste and see the goodness of the Lord' (cf. Ps. 34:9).

Presence is the land of eternal childhood. In Presence, we grow ever-younger, never older. Presence 'satisfies us with good as long as we live so that our youth is renewed like the eagle's' (cf. Ps. 103:5).

Presence is the virginal point of the Now in which time and space disappear.[32] In Presence, we traverse the indefinable boundary between time and eternity. In Presence, we realize that 'now is the acceptable time, now is the day of salvation' (cf. 2 Cor. 6:2).

Presence is a distancing from the other allowing intimacy to arise. In Presence, we afford 'space' to others, causing them to appreciate our respectfulness and draw near to us in spirit. Presence is the perfect synergy of Jesus saying: 'Come to me and I will give you rest' (cf. Mt. 11:28) and 'Do not cling to me' (cf. Jn. 20:17).

---

[32] See my book, *Le Point Vierge: Meditations on the Mystery of Presence.*

Presence is an inherently *kenotic* mystery. Presence is a detachment from self that is also its glorious self-fulfillment. In Presence, we apprehend that Jesus 'did not deem equality with God something to be grasped at' and so 'was highly exalted him and given the name which is above every name' (cf. Phil. 2:6-9).

Presence is an inner poverty that becomes infinite wealth. In Presence, we learn to 'not store up for yourselves treasures on earth, where moth and decay destroy, and thieves break in and steal, but in heaven, where neither moth nor decay destroys, nor thieves break in and steal' (cf. Mt. 6:19–20).

The freedom of the Holy Spirit to 'blow whither he will' (cf. Jn. 3:8) and to distribute gifts as he will (cf. 1 Cor. 12:11) arises from the relinquishment of Father and Son, both of whom refuse to be understood in terms other than self-emptying. In Presence, we partake of the eternal, inner-trinitarian self-giving of God.

Presence is a transfiguring Light that engenders awe and bliss. Once in Presence, we never want to leave. In Presence, we echo the words of St. Peter on Mt. Tabor: 'Lord, it is good for us to be here! Let us pitch some tents and abide here with you forever!' (cf. Lk. 9:33).

In Presence, the notion of 'never' has no meaning. In Presence, there is always only Now. In Presence, we are 'born anew' in every moment (cf. Jn. 3:3-7). In Presence, we are always becoming 'a new creation in Christ' (cf. 2 Cor. 5:17).

In Presence, we stand in awe before the mystery of being. Presence reveals us as *homo adorans* - those who kneel in adoring awareness of an ineffable Source greater than ourselves. Presence is the intuitive realization that in God 'we live and move and have our being' (cf. Acts 17:28).

In Presence, we realize that our bodies are essentially food for worms, that 'we are dust and unto dust we must return' (cf. Sir. 3:20). At the same time, we realize, with joy, that in acknowledging our finitude, we 'have already passed from death to life' (cf. Jn. 5:24).

Presence is a mystery that is always possessed and given away. We give ourselves to others in Presence because we are possessed of Presence. In Presence, we mirror the Trinity whose infinite blessedness lies in both giving and receiving both the gift and the giver.

Presence is the redemption of guilt, shame and regret. Presence is the graveyard of fears, doubts and insecurities. In Presence, we 'will not be put to shame and the world's reproaches we will remember no more' (cf. Isa. 54:4).

In Presence, we are 'naked without shame' (cf. Gen. 2:25). In Presence, we re-enter the Garden of Paradise, surrendering our egoic 'knowledge of good and evil' and our idolatrous need to 'be as God' (cf. Gen. 3:5).

Presence is the fullness of the *Plérōma* piercing the veil from eternity into history. In Presence, the world is bathed in the glow of 'the heavenly Jerusalem' (cf. Rev. 21:2; Heb. 12:22). Presence is the teleological 8th day of re-creation in which 'the Lamb of God is himself the light' (cf. Rev. 21:23).

Presence reveals history as held and made perfect by a Love so *plérōmic* as to make what we call 'evil' ultimately irrelevant. 'Everything works for good' for those who abide in Presence (cf. Rom. 8:28; Prv. 24:20).

It sounds insensitive to say that Presence reveals evil to be nothing more than an illusion of the mind, but so it is. When we dwell intentionally in Presence, we awaken to the realization that, in God, 'all is well and all manner of things shall be well'.[33]

Presence reveals the world perfect in every way, perfect at every moment. All comes from Presence, all returns to Presence, perfectly 'achieving the purpose' for which it is, i.e., for the manifestation and glorification of its self-exteriorizing Source (cf. Isa. 55:11).

One moment of living in Presence releases more healing goodness into the cosmos than a lifetime of social engineering. Nothing done apart from Presence 'bears fruit that will last' (cf. Jn. 15:2, 16).

---

[33] Julian of Norwich, *Revelations of Divine Love.*

Babbling about Presence - apart from saying nothing at all - is the only way to give it adequate expression. Hyperbole is the grammar of Presence. Transfigured in light of Presence, we 'hardly know what to say' (cf. Mk. 9:6).

Presence is the existential equivalent of the ancient *Shekinah* of God. In Presence, we enter a *Cloud of Unknowing*[34] in which we are given a wisdom 'which none of our adversaries will be able to withstand or contradict' (cf. Lk. 21:15).

Presence is the pre-condition for all that is said or done. Inspired words and actions emerge unbidden from the mystery of Presence. 'Even before a word is on our tongues,' it is beheld, as it were, in Presence (cf. Ps. 139:4).

Presence is often pictured as an aura, a halo or a *penumbra*. These signify the inherent ungraspableness of Presence. In the light of Presence 'we see light' (cf. Ps. 36:9), yet Presence itself is nowhere to be seen.

In Presence, we realize that 'nothing that is real can be threatened, and nothing unreal exists'.[35] In Presence, we 'know the truth and the truth sets us free' (cf. Jn. 8:32). Presence liberates us from our 'slavery to the fear of death' (cf. Heb. 2:15).

---

[34] *The Cloud of Unknowing* is a 14th century mystical tract from an anonymous source, instructing the reader on apophatic theology and contemplative prayer.
[35] Opening statement and governing assumption of *Course in Miracles*.

Because it is a privation, evil enjoys no substance, no reality. The problem is, the whole world is hypnotized by it (cf. Rev. 12:9). The whole world is in the power of the Evil One' 'the Deceiver' (cf. 1 Jn. 5:19; Jn. 8:44).

The deeper we enter into Presence, the sillier our questions become. The more we abide in Presence, the less need we feel 'to ask any questions' (cf. Lk. 20:40).

Presence conquers our fears, doubts and insecurities by subversion, but not through head-on assault. In Presence, we refuse to 'fight evil with evil' but we 'overcome evil with good' (cf. Rom. 12:21).

Presence is not in competition with anyone or anything. In Presence, we transcend all dualities, antinomies, dialectics. Presence obviates argumentation and imparts a 'peace that passes all understanding' (cf. Php. 4:7)

Presence is the power that allows thinking to peter itself out. Presence is our acknowledgment to God that 'Your ways are not our ways, our thoughts are not Your thoughts' (cf. Isa. 55:8-9; Ezek. 18:25).

Presence is the compassionate matron who allows kicking and crying children to fall asleep in her embrace. 'Even if such a mother could forget her child' (cf. Isa. 49:15), Presence will never fail to comfort those enfolded in it.

Presence is the graveyard where drama and histrionics go to die. Presence is the sound of silence in which the cries of the anxious receive no response. Peace is found, 'not in the earthquake, not in the fire but in the still small voice' of Presence (cf. 1 Kg. 19:11–12).

Presence is the oven in which the yeast of our transcendence turns the dough of our lives into 'the bread of life' (cf. Jn. 6:48). The bread is given 'for the life of the world' (cf. Jn. 6:51).

Everything arises afresh in the mystery of Presence. Presence is the pristine garden in which seeds of contemplation sprout continuously as flowers of beauty, goodness and bliss. The sweet scent from this 'garden of God' (cf. 1 Cor. 3:9) exudes from those who abide in Presence.

Presence is the silence of the Lamb (cf. Isa. 53:7). Presence is Jesus standing alone and self-possessed before Pilate (cf. Jn. 19:5-9). Presence opens, as were, 'the seventh seal', generating 'silence in heaven' (cf. Rev. 8:1).

Presence is wordless, thoughtless consciousness, perfectly alert yet devoid of analysis.

Presence is unrestricted openness to the totality of being, without itself being a part of existence. Presence is a participation in the aseity of God who is at once immanent and transcendent vis-a-vis the world he has made.

Presence is a participation in the joy of Jesus: 'I thank you, Father, Lord of heaven and earth, that you have hidden these things from the wise and understanding and revealed them to the merest children' (cf. Mt. 11:25).

If the word 'Presence' were used instead of the word 'God,' it would perhaps be easier to glimpse the Mystery towards which the word 'God' points. Though 'God' sometimes seems remote or absent, Presence is 'with us always, even to the end of the age' (cf. Mt. 28:20).

Presence produces fruit within us without any help from us. Like seed scattered by a divine sower, Presence 'produces of itself, first the blade, then the ear, then the full grain in the ear'. Presence makes it possible for us to blossom like 'the greatest of all shrubs, putting forth large branches, so that the birds of the air can make nests in our shade' (cf. Mk. 4:32).

The instant we shift from thinking to being present, Presence transforms us into instruments of peace, simplicity and beauty. In Presence, we wonder, 'What shall we render to the Lord for his infinite bounty to us?' (Ps. 116:12).

Presence is the nowhere place from whence inspiration comes. In Presence, we don't know whether we are 'in the body or out of the body'. Presence is the 'third heaven' where we 'hear things that can neither be told nor uttered' (cf. 2 Cor. 12:2-4).

Presence as the precondition for breakthrough change. Presence is the divine interval in which 'change of heart' takes place.[36] No one comes to God, but by abiding in Presence (cf. Jn. 14:6).

In Presence, we discover that our *desire* to love is purer and more transformative than our *acts* of love (cf. Rom. 7:19-20). When we give to others from Presence, we find that we 'have put in more than all the others' (cf. Lk. 21:3).

Erotic love is not a lower form of love or a distant parable for God's love, but a natural orientation towards the transcendent finding its purification and perfection in Presence. In Presence, we see every person as 'my delight, my espoused' (cf. Isa. 62:4; Song 7:6).

Natural, human love can be a point of departure into Presence. Sexual union intimates a more transcendent, yet no less ecstatic, communion with God in Presence. In Presence, we discover a Spouse who 'ravishes our hearts with a glance of his eyes' (cf. Song 4:9).

In his eternal trinitarian mystery, God already possesses a nuptial form. In Presence, we are assimilated into God's trinitarian communion, not as prurient by-standers but as 'of one heart and soul, possessing everything in common' with God (cf. Acts 4:32).

---

[36] A better translation of 'repentance' is 'change of heart'. See, e.g., David Bentley Hart's translation of Mk. 1:15 in his book *The New Testament: A Translation*.

The Trinity is a Mystery of infinite, self-giving Love. In Presence, we partake of the self-divestment of God. In Presence, we share in God's joy (cf. Jn. 15:11) 'giving all that we have' (cf. Lk. 21:4), knowing we possess 'nothing that we have not received' (cf. 1 Cor. 4:7)

Because alterity - difference, 'distance,' otherness' - exists in God himself as Trinity, God is free to create something different from himself which acquires from him its beauty of being 'other'. In Presence, we discover that 'unity differentiates, and perfect unity differentiates perfectly'.

Presence is an apprehension filled with wonder, awe and freedom. Knowledge, by contrast, is method, analysis and necessity. In Presence, we come to understand that 'the wisdom of the world is foolishness with God' (cf. 1 Cor. 3:19).

Approached for knowledge, the world appears as a monstrous mechanism, blankly silent about its meaning and its purpose. Approached in Presence, the world is a revelation of 'the glory of God, radiant as a most rare jewel' (cf. Rev. 21:11). In Presence, the cosmos is an unveiling of beauty of the Infinite.[37]

In Presence, we learn what it means to say, 'I cannot not love'. In Presence, our freedom to misbehave becomes the necessity to show compassion. In Presence, we never 'withhold good from others when it is in our power to do it. (cf. Prv. 3:27).

---

[37] For an elaboration of this theme, see David Bentley Hart, *The Beauty of the Infinite: The Aesthetics of Christian Truth*.

Presence refines our desire for love. Presence turns possessiveness into benignity, and craving into affection. Presence introduces a holy relinquishment into our desire to love and to be loved. In Presence, we learn to love as Jacob loved Rachel (cf. Gen. 29:21-31).

Sitting with another in Presence bonds us more completely than any tangible expression of affection. Presence divinizes every human gesture of love. In Presence, like Tobit, we embrace others, not 'because of lust, but with sincerity' (cf. Tobit 8:7).

Presence is devoid of expectation, anticipation, trepidation and calculation. Presence is the space where an intuitive, inexpressible wisdom is given. In Presence, we are immersed in transcendental truth, the 'truth that sets us free' (cf. Jn. 8:32).

Presence envelops us in our woundedness like a mother whimpering child. Presence whispers gentle assurances to our disquieted minds and hearts. In Presence, we hear the voice of Christ, 'Fear not, it is I' (cf. Jn. 6:20).

Our individual uniqueness does not disappear in Presence. In Presence, we remain incommunicable persons in unsubstitutable alterity. In Presence, we acquire a fresh appreciation that 'we are wonderfully made' (cf. Ps. 139:14; 2 Chr. 26:15).

Presence dismantles our character armor and disarms us of our protective shields. In Presence, we face reality with the same defenseless confidence that David shed 'his sword and his armor' and approached his adversary armed with nothing but 'the name of the Lord' (1 Sam. 17:39–40).

Presence subverts our resistance to reality, and dispels our objections to the so-called 'unfairness' of life. In Presence, we know that 'all God's work is perfect and all his ways are just (Dt. 32:4).

Presence makes forgiveness immediate, infinite and irrelevant. Presence precedes forgiveness just as the prodigal father's unconditional love preceded and rendered unnecessary his son's prepared confession (cf. Lk. 15:17-24).

When we are present to anyone or anything, a space is created where communion becomes possible. In Presence, we are one with Jesus who 'sat down beside the well' and entered into communion with a woman of Samaria. Meeting another in Presence, it's as if we have been 'given living water welling up to eternal life' (cf. Jn. 4:10–15).

In Presence, no situation is dire. In Presence, we lose our tragic sense of life. In Presence, we say with Job - but with much more mirth - 'yet though he slay me, I know my Redeemer lives' (cf. Job 13:15; 19:25).

Hope and joy arise naturally in Presence. The advent of Presence promises redemption even under the most unfortunate circumstances. In Presence, we know 'nothing is impossible for God' (cf. Lk. 1:37; cf. Jer. 32:17).

Presence is the space of personal integration. Presence strips us of egoic personae, leading us into *'who'* we are apart from *'what'* we are. In Presence, we glimpse our true identity as 'hidden with Christ in God' (cf. Col. 3:3).

In Presence, neither doubts nor fears, qualms nor questions arise. In Presence, an epiphany of being occurs that seems like a perpetual first 'big bang of creation'.

Time and space exist only outside of Presence. In Presence, it's as if 'the sky vanishes like a scroll that is rolled up, and every mountain and island is removed from its place' (Rev. 6:14). Even the angels move aside when they see us walking in Presence.

Persons living in Presence project a benign indifference to the problems of the world, yet exhibit deep compassion for those who are suffering. Because they are in possession of the peace 'the world cannot give' (cf. Jn. 14:27) they, like Christ, are grieved at those whose hearts are hardened (cf. Mk. 3:5).

Abiding in Presence, we see the futility of trying to 'change the world'. We know that Presence is the only world where we truly live. In Presence, we learn to live 'in the world but not be of the world' (cf. Jn. 15:19).

Presence is 'the pearl of great price' (cf. Mt. 13:46). Those who have found it forsake all else to possess it.

Presence always arises as something of a miracle, an epiphany, a revelation. When we awaken to Presence as the Source of our own capacity to be present, we exclaim: 'In your Light, O God, we see light' (Ps. 36:9).

Only effusive hyperbole, aphoristic paradox, effusive rhetoric or absolute silence is appropriate to the mystery of Presence. In Presence, we are rendered at once mute and ecstatic. Like the apostles on Mt. Tabor, we 'do not know what to say' (cf. Lk. 9:33; Mt. 20:22).

In Presence, we acquire the virginal attentiveness of the wise virgins awaiting the appearance of their beloved bridegroom (cf. Mt. 21:1ff.). In Presence, we acquire 'the eyes of servants look to the hand of their master, or the eyes of a maid on the hand of her mistress' (Ps. 123:2).

Presence is the fulcrum with which Archimedes claimed he could lift the world. Presence is the power with which Christ 'lifts up' the world to the Father through his death, resurrection and ascension (cf. Jn. 12:32; 13:3).

Presence is a seamless, simultaneous mystery of 'letting go' and 'lifting up'. Presence is at once the descent of self-emptying and and the arising of self-fulfillment. In Presence, we find ourselves on Jacob's ladder, beholding 'the angels of God ascending and descending upon it!' (Gen. 28:12).

In Presence, we see our thoughts and actions more clearly. In Presence, we perceive ourselves from a standpoint beyond ourselves. In Presence, we acquire a share 'in the mind of Christ' (cf. 1 Cor. 2:16).

Presence suggests an answer to the most fundamental philosophical question, 'Why is there something rather than nothing?'. In Presence, we apprehend that only an infinite Wellspring of freedom and love - i.e., 'God' - can account for our existence. In Presence, we intuitively grasp that 'in him all things hold together' (cf. Col. 1:16–17).

In Presence, we open ourselves to others, not by complying with some heteronomous requirement but because of the 'image and likeness of God' operative within us. In Presence, we participate in the life of the Trinity which is a fontal Mystery of triune personal openness (cf. Jn. 8:29; Mk. 9:7).

In Presence, we see that dying is our final act of pure self-surrender in which we allow ourselves to be taken into the *Plērōma* of God. Presence allows us to use our final breath to say, with Christ, 'into your hands, Father, I commend my spirit' (cf. Lk. 23:46).

In Presence, differences do not become divisions, polarities do not devolve into polemics. Presence shows us that the world, in all its variegated diversity and, indeed, in its very 'otherness' from God, is, 'very, very good' (cf. Gen, 1:31).

In Presence, we are not annihilated in an Advaita-like state of pantheistic non-differentiation, but are 'un-selved' in Christ only to rise with him in a new life we recognize as our true self. In Presence, we are, as it were, 'crucified with Christ' such that we realize 'it is no longer we who live, but Christ who lives in us; and the life we now live is one with the Son of God, who loved us and gave himself for us' (Gal 2:20).

Presence is a space of healing where we, suffering from our 'slavery to sin and the fear of death' (cf. Heb. 2:15) experience an inner release from the bondage of our evil thoughts (cf. Mt. 15:19) and receive a taste of the 'freedom of the children of God' (cf. Rom. 8:21).

Everything is capable of experiencing and manifesting Presence in accord with its own nature. Each created object enjoys its own measure of self-presence. 'Sun and moon, rain and dew, fire and heat' - the whole of creation - 'declares the glory of God' (cf. Dan. 3:28-68; Ps. 19:1-4).

Presence allows us to see the aliveness of nature. In Presence, we understand how it's possible, as Annie Dillard says and Jesus implies (cf. Lk. 19:40), even to teach a stone to talk.[38]

---

[38] Annie Dillard, *Teaching a Stone to Talk*.

The Mystery of Presence shows itself most visibly in our capacity for *self*-presence. Our experience of self-transcendence reveals both our identity with, and difference from, the triune God who possesses us (cf. Gen. 1:26; Isa. 55:9).

Our experience of ourselves as *persons* is the manifestation of Presence within us. Presence is the fontal Source of all that is personal. In Presence, we are astonished that *who* we are as persons precedes and makes possible *what* we are human beings (cf. Isa. 62:2; Rev. 2:17).

Presence makes our encounters even with so-called inanimate matter quasi-personal. Is this not why St. Francis could speak with such love to 'sister moon and brother sun'?

Presence is the redemption of all that is placed within it. Thoughts and feelings are redeemed in Presence just as much as is a tragic car accident. In Presence, 'we destroy arguments and every proud obstacle to the knowledge of God, and take every thought captive to obey Christ' (cf. 2 Cor. 10:5).

Placed in Presence, the pain and suffering of life's countless disappointments is drawn out from us as if from a sore body in a hot bath of Epsom salts. In Presence, we resemble Naaman, the Syrian, who, at the word of the prophet, Elisha, 'plunged himself seven times in the river Jordan, and his flesh was restored like that of a little child, and he was made clean' (cf. 2 Kg. 5:14).

Presence reveals being and knowing as coincident in a single Source greater than both. Presence is a participation in the *Sophia* of God (cf. Prv. 8:22ff.) which is the connective tissue, so to speak, between our epistemic and ontic dimensions as the 'image and likeness' of the God in whom knowing, being, and acting are one.

Presence is our gravitational center point. In Presence, we sink into our deepest center and are lifted up into the kingdom of God. Abiding in Presence as the virginal center point of our being, we experience 'the weight of glory' (cf. 2 Cor. 4:17). Actions issuing from Presence are resplendent with gravitas.

In Presence, we are equipoised upon an internal spiritual fulcrum which, like that of Archimedes, can elevate the universe. Presence is the same power flowing through us that carries the cosmos, using us as its lever, into an ever-more-perfect synergy with its Creator.

Presence is our sacred portal into the kingdom of God. But as Jesus says of this point of entrée: 'The gate is narrow and the way is hard, that leads to life, and those who find it are few' (cf. Mt. 7:14).

Presence is hidden in plain sight. Many there are, however, who 'have eyes, but see not, who have ears, but never understand' (cf. Jer. 5:21; Mt. 13:14).

Presence is an interior, sophianic leading us ever more deeply into the present moment. Presence is the kindly light of God[39] that draws us ever forward, dispelling the darkness that seems to threaten (cf. Jn. 1:5; 2 Cor. 6:14).

Silence is the language of Presence. Abiding in the 'cave of the heart,'[40] we hear 'the small still voice' of God (cf. 2 Kg. 19:12).

Silence is at once the condition for and result of Presence. In Presence, we are reduced to silence. In Presence, we are with 'the Lord in his holy temple' and 'all the earth keeps silence before him' (cf. Hab. 2:20).

Stillness pervades and encompasses all that is. In Presence, stillness speaks.[41]

The closest we can come to God in this world is to experience Presence. In Presence, we enter the Cloud of Unknowing (cf. Ex. 40:34) where, like Moses, we see God face-to-face (cf. Ex. 33:11). In Presence, our own faces are made incandescent with God's transfiguring light (cf. Ex. 34:33).

Presence is the manifestation of the the risen Christ, perfect in love, who 'casts out all fear' (cf. 1 Jn. 4:18) and expels our demons (cf. Lk. 4:35).

---

[39] John Henry Newman, *Lead Kindly Light*.

[40] See Shirley Du Boulay, *The Cave of the Heart: The Life of Swami Abhishiktananda*.

[41] Eckhart Tolle, *Stillness Speaks*.

Presence is the destruction of our egoic existence. In Presence, God rescues us from our towers of Babel (cf. Gen. 11:4ff.) and ushers us into his heavenly Jerusalem (cf. Rev. 21:2; Heb. 12:22).

Ego is a cocoon of unconsciousness that keeps us somnambulant. Presence transforms us from human caterpillars into human butterflies. In Presence, we fly as free as 'birds of the air,' held aloft by the Spirit of God (cf. Mt. 6:26).

Presence is at once our own deepest personal identity and a Power that precedes and exceeds it. In Presence, 'it is no longer we who live, but God who lives in us' (cf. Gal. 2:20). In Presence, 'we live and move and have our being' (cf. Acts 17:28).

Presence deepens our temporal experience, even as it drains us of its drama. In Presence, we are 'in the world but not of it' (cf. Jn. 15:19). In Presence, we are intoxicated by the Spirit (cf. Acts 2:13) yet sober as a judge.

Presence neutralizes our anxiety and bathes life in an indefinably benevolent light. Presence takes the edge off of evil, allowing us to see it for what it is, i.e. an illusion of the egoic mind. In Presence, 'no evil shall befall you, no scourge come near your tent' (cf. Ps. 91:10).

Presence ushers us into a world beyond good and evil. Presence is a power that transcends morality while imparting a connaturality for doing what's good. In Presence, 'our righteousness exceeds that of the Pharisees and the scribes' (cf. Mt. 5:20).

Presence delivers what ethics can never attain. In Presence, we 'are saved by faith, not by works' (cf. Gal. 2:16). In Presence, we have nothing to boast about except our weakness (cf. 2 Cor. 12:9).

Presence is arresting. Presence stops us in our tracks. In Presence, our fears, misgivings and insecurities are banished as quickly as those of Thomas. In Presence, we declare, 'My Lord and my God!' (cf. Jn. 20:26-28).

In Presence, we can calm a crisis with a simple look. Abiding in Presence, we can defuse anger with a simple softening of our eyes (cf. Prv. 15:1; Mt. 10:21).

Presence disarms us of our sins and sets us free from our 'slavery to the fear of death

(cf. Heb. 2:15). Presence is the power of the risen Christ, 'bearing our griefs and carrying our sorrows'. In Presence, Christ arises to take upon himself 'the chastisements that make us whole' (cf. Isa. 53:4-5).

Presence and self-possession go hand-in-hand. In Presence, our true self is not lost, but found. In Presence, we are prodigal sons and daughters (cf. Lk. 15:11ff.), the stray sheep (cf. Mt. 18:12ff.), and the missing coins (cf. Lk. 15:8ff.) which once 'were lost but now are found'.

Christ abides anonymously in the mystery of Presence. In Presence, we realize that 'whatever we do to the least of these' we do to him (cf. Mt. 25:40).

Presence is the true fountain of youth. Those who practice Presence always grow younger, never older. In Presence, 'our youth is renewed like the eagle's' (cf. Ps. 103:5).

Presence is a bottomless wellspring of inspiration. Those who think or write, speak or act from Presence do so with a voice and a style more graceful than their own. In Presence, we share in the *dynamis* of Christ who 'spoke as one with authority', unlike that of the scribes and the Pharisees (cf. Mk. 1:22).

Presence takes possession of us as instruments of God's redemptive design. In Presence, we need 'not be anxious about how we are to speak or what we are to say; for what we are to say will be given to us in that hour' (cf. Mt. 10:19).

Those who practice Presence embody the desire of the poet: 'I am a hole in a flute through which the Christ's breath moves - listen to this music'.[42]

Poise is of a piece with Presence. In Presence, we are as poised, hyper-aware and discerning as a 'deer secure upon the heights' (cf. Ps. 18:33). In Presence, we are alert with the attentive heart of a lover listening for 'the voice of the beloved' (Sg. 28).

Presence is the selfless communication of what is ours, and the selfless welcoming of what is other from ourselves. Presence is the perfect enactment of Christ's words, 'May they be one, Father, as you and I are one' (cf. Jn. 17:21).

God's trinitarian life is an unceasing, ever-more-ecstatic flowing of the Divine Persons from one another to one another and in one another (cf. Jn. 14:11). In Presence, we are mystically assimilated into the reciprocal, ineffable self-surrender of the Father and the Son.

If Presence is the deepest Source of our existence, then divine bliss is our natural state of being. Could this be the inner, existential meaning of Jesus' desire 'that my joy may be in you, and that your joy may be full'? (cf. Jn. 15:11).

---

[42] Hafiz, *The Gift.*

It's impossible to be in Presence and not be infused with joy. In Presence, we exclaim with Christ: "We thank you, Lord God, that you have hidden these things from the wise and understanding and revealed them to those of childlike receptivity' (cf. Mt. 11:25).

Presence takes us beyond the ethical dilemmas that bedevil our understanding. In Presence, we rise above debates about good vs. evil, right vs. wrong. Instead, we see, to our astonished relief, that 'God makes his sun rise on the evil and on the good, and sends rain on the just and on the unjust' (cf. Mt. 5:45).

Presence prohibits argument and debate. Presence disarms us of our propensity for polarization. In Presence, we learn to 'love our enemies and do good to those who hate us'. In Presence, we find it increasingly possible 'to bless those who curse us, and pray for those who abuse us' (cf. Lk. 6:27–28; cf. 1 Cor. 4:12).

In Presence, we stop playing the world's game of tit-for-tat. We escape the cul-de-sac of 'an eye for an eye, a tooth for a tooth' (cf. Dt. 19:21; Mt. 5:38). In Presence, we experience 'the peace of God that surpasses all understanding' (cf. Php. 4:7) and which produces the 'fruits of the Holy Spirit' (cf. Gal. 5:22-23).

To close ourselves off from others is to go against the law of love that underpins us. To refuse to love is struggling uselessly against the current of God's desire (cf. Acts 26:14). In Presence, we relax into the arms of Christ who summons us, 'Come to me, all you who are weary and heavy laden, and I will give you rest' (cf. Mt. 11:28).

Those who enter Presence do so as those entering a cool cathedral. The enormity, beauty and sacred stillness of Presence makes us forget the heated, petty world left at the door. Entering Presence, we become aware that we 'are the temple of God' (cf. 1 Cor, 3:16)), the 'dwelling place' of God's glory (cf. Eph. 2:22).

Moving from thinking to Presence is the simplest, yet most subtle and difficult shift a person can make. Listening to the voices in our heads, we are 'thinking as human beings do, not as God does' (cf. Mt. 16:23). Presence 'imparts the secret and hidden wisdom of God, which God decreed before the ages for our glorification' (cf. 1 Cor. 2:7).

Presence reveals the world of fear-filled impetuousness - of plans, schedules, deadlines and built-in expectations - as a house of cards and a pack of lies. In Presence, we hear the words of Christ, 'Come apart by yourselves to a solitary place and rest for a while' (cf. Mk. 6:31).

Building our house on anything other than Presence is 'building on sand'. When the winds of the world 'blow and beat against our house it will fall, and great will be the collapse' (cf. Mt. 7:26-27).

In Presence, the world seems a kaleidoscope of ever-changing, ever-more-beautiful horizons 'in which we live and move and have our being' (cf. Acts 17:28). When, in Presence, we 'look at the heavens, the work of God's hands, the moon and the stars which God has established, we wonder: 'What are we, O God, that you are mindful of us, that you care so much for us?!' (cf. Ps. 8:3–4).

Presence is the permanent, ever-present oasis to which we can retreat when trudging doggedly through the desert of life. In Presence, it's as if, 'tired from the journey,' we join Jesus as Jacob's well and say to him, 'Give us a drink' (cf. Jn. 4:6-7).

Presence saves us from getting overheated during the demands and routines of the workaday world. The moment we enter Presence, 'the fever leaves us' (cf. Lk. 4:39).

Presence reveals death to be neither the opposite nor the equal of life but its siamese twin. Presence is simultaneously a death and a resurrection. Whenever we die to self-interest we rise to new life, the life we enjoy with God 'since before the foundation of the world' (cf. Jn. 17:24; Eph. 1:4; 1 Pt. 1:20).

Presence is the manifestation of the' final, cosmic *Plērōma* within the conditions of time and space. In Presence, we intuit the power of the One who is 'before all things' and in whom 'all things hold together' (cf. Col. 1:17).

Presence is the experience of the end in the beginning and the beginning in the end. In Presence, it's as if the 'acorn and oak' reveal themselves in stereoscopic harmony. In Presence, we glimpse 'the Alpha and the Omega', the One who is and who was and who is to come' (cf. Rev. 1:8).

Presence is an anticipatory fullness of that for which we insatiably yearn. In Presence, we receive a sampling of 'the living water' flowing from an eternal 'spring within us, welling up to eternal life' (cf. Jn. 4:14).

In Presence, we intuit an ultimate ecstasy within the agonistic movements of concrete existence. In Presence, we apprehend an eschatological splendor within our world of death and destruction. Because of the joy Presence portends, we 'gladly embrace the cross' (cf. Heb. 12:2).

Presence alights from an indefinable still point[43] within us that is at once the epicenter and circumference of our lives. In Presence, a 'gentle silence envelops' us in which God's all-powerful Word leaps from heaven, from his royal throne' and 'makes his home' within us (cf. Wis. 18:14-15; Jn. 14:23).

Presence can be experienced but never thought. Presence is real but never objective. Presence is an extension of God's own Wisdom (*Sophia*), a mystery 'more mobile than any motion, and, because of its pureness, pervades and penetrates all things (cf. Wis. 7:24).

Presence melts our defenses and softens our eyes and hearts. Presence relaxes our grip on life. In Presence, we find 'rest for our souls' (cf. Mt. 11:29) and escape 'hardness of heart' (cf. Mk. 10:5).

---

[43] See William Johnston, S.J. *The Still Point: Reflections on Zen and Christian Mysticism.* See also T. S. Eliot, *Four Quartets: Burnt Norton.*

Presence is the space in which we let go and discover the truth about ourselves. Presence is the space of *Gelassenheit* (relinquishment) in which all things appear as they are, not as we would have them. Presence 'fastens your belts for us and carries us where we do not wish to go' (cf. Jn. 21:18).

Presence reveals the transcendental nature of our true identity. In Presence, we are empowered 'to do the good we want to do, and avoid the evil we do not want to do' (cf. Rom. 7:19).

In Presence, we learn to disidentify with any and all definitions of ourselves. In Presence, we see that our 'lives are hidden with Christ in God' (Col. 3:3).

In Presence, it is impossible for us to politicize. Presence reveals every form of national, racial, ideological, sexual identification to be sin. In Presence, 'there is neither Jew nor Greek, neither slave nor free, neither male nor female; for we are all one in Christ Jesus' (cf. Gal. 3:27–28).

God is a primordial Mystery of self-dis-identifcation, an aboriginal Mystery of self-transcendence, an ineffable Source of ungraspable Presence. In Presence, we dis-identify with personal identification, mirroring and partaking of God's own self-effacement (cf. 2 Pt. 1:4).

What Christians call 'Trinity' is the God who transcends Himself within Himself. Our experience of Presence is a participation in the self-transcending - and therefore self-dis-identification - of Father, Son, and Holy Spirit.

The Father (Source) transcends Himself eternally in the begetting of the Son (Word). The Son 'does not deem equality with God (Source) as something to be grasped at but empties himself' in an act of self-transcendence mirroring that of the Father (cf. Phil. 2:6-11). The mutual self-surrender of Father (Source) and Son (Word) issues forth in a *Penumbra* of Presence (Spirit), enfolding and perfecting this primordial Mystery of self-transcendence. Our ability to stand outside ourselves within ourselves (cf. Rom. 7:6-19) is the Presence of God operating salvifically within us.

Presence delivers us from the wasteland of morality and ethics. Ethics is what fills the vacuum when Presence is missing. In Presence, we need no guidance about the right thing to do or say. In Presence, wisdom replaces deliberation with an intuition that supersedes calculation (cf. Prv. 14:6; Wis. 21:18).

In Presence, we experience a rebirth of childlike innocence infused with an arresting depth of discernment. Presence imbues us with eternal youth and ancient wisdom. In Presence, we become 'as wise as serpents and as innocent as doves' (cf. Mt. 10:16).

Presence acts as an internal governor upon our impulses and actions. Presence is the 'aboriginal voice of Christ within us',[44] reminding us that we 'do not live by bread alone' (cf. Lk. 4:4).

Presence neutralizes the chatter in our heads and unveils the wisdom of the heart. Presence cautions us to pause until we see the truth, and compels us to act once we do. Presence saves us from the vagaries of the gnomic (deliberative) will, i.e., from 'eating from the poisonous tree of the (presumed) knowledge of good and evil' (cf. Gen. 2:16-17).

Presence engenders infinite compassion. Immersed in Presence, we see clearly that God's 'rain falls on the good and bad alike, and God's light bathes the just and unjust' equally in its uncreated splendor (cf. Mt. 5:45).

Viewed in the light of Presence, every person appears beautiful. Presence turns criticism into kindness, judgment into understanding. In Presence, we are rendered incapable of 'throwing the first stone' (cf. Jn. 8:7).

In Presence, we painfully discern the lack of Presence in ourselves and others, without, however, experiencing the slightest judgment or condemnation. In Presence, we experience the compassion of Christ who says, 'Father, forgive them, they know not what they do' (cf. Lk. 23:34)

---

[44] The phrase used by John Henry Newman to describe the voice of conscience. See *Catechism of the Catholic Church* #1778.

Presence is at once intimate and infinite, immediate but without beginning or end. Presence is an experience of the risen Christ 'the same yesterday, today, and forever' (cf. Heb. 13:8).

In Presence, we experience the unconditioned act of our existence as coming from a Source that is both immanent and transcendent. In Presence, we come to know God 'as the first and the last' (cf. Isa. 41:4), our 'beginning and our end' (cf. Rev. 22:13).

It was Christ's intimate, immediate experience of the Presence of his Father that caused him to exclaim, 'the Father and I are one' (cf. Jn. 10:30) and 'the Father is greater than I' (cf. Jn. 14:28). In Presence, we experience by grace what Jesus experienced by nature.[45]

Presence is God's house of mercy (cf. Lk. 10:35). Presence is the 'dwelling place of God' (cf. Eph. 2:22) in which no kettle ever calls any pot black (cf. Song 1:5). Presence is the crystal palace of God (cf. Rev. 15:2) where no one throws stones (cf. Jn. 8:7).

Presence is our elusive point of connection between our life and the life of God within us. Presence arises from in the 'deepest center'[46] of our existence where we are hypostatically united with God, inseparable yet unconfused.

---

[45] The consensus of the early church fathers is that through *theosis* (i.e., deification, cf. 2 Pt. 1:4), we 'become by grace what God is by nature'.

[46] See St. John of the Cross, *Living Flame of Love, Stanza 1*.

Presence is electric with the power of actuality. Abiding in Presence, we experience the absolute priority of 'I Am' (cf. Ex. 3:14). In Presence, we experience the ontological difference between '*who*' we are as the pre-eternal sons and daughters of God and '*what*' we are as persons inhering in human nature.

Presence is our existential apprehension of the Infinite. Presence is an apperception that is at once immediate and transcendent. In Presence, we experience God as *Emmanuel*, God-with-us (cf. Mt. 1:23) and God as *Non aliud* (Not other) (cf. Ps. 135:5).

The reality of Presence is hidden from those who have not made the shift from thinking to the conscious experience of simple, limpid, spacious awareness. Inhabiting external reality apart from Presence, we 'have eyes but do not see, ears but do not hear' (Ps. 115:5; cf. Mk. 8:18).

Presence is devoid of ideas but filled with attentiveness. Presence is poise on steroids. In Presence, we are filled with ecstatic joy as we experience our 'absolute dependence'[47] upon a Source greater than, distinct from, yet one with ourselves.

Presence is an existential intuition of the unnameable, transcendent, unconditioned Origin of our existence. This Source is, so to say, the 'Father' of every created being, dependent on none but lovingly, sustainingly present to all (cf. Ps. 139:7).

---

[47] The famous phrase used by Friedrich Schleiermacher to describe this same dynamic.

Jesus says, 'I AM the Way, the Truth and the Life' (cf. Jn. 14:6). But what if he meant: 'I AM' *is* the Way, the Truth and the Life? If this is the case, then our 'I-am-ness' is a divinizing participation in the One who calls himself 'I AM'. We are 'they who are' *in* Him 'who is I AM'.

The 'is-ing-ness' of things awakens us to the mystery of Presence. Presence is the answer to the perennial philosophical question, 'Why is there something rather than nothing?' In Presence alone we grasp the miracle of creation *ex nihilo*.

Presence reveals that there is no such thing as nothing. 'Nothing' does not, cannot 'exist'. Every so-called 'absence' is but another form of Presence. Every so-called 'evil' is a bedeviling deception quickly expelled once its lies are named and tamed (cf. Mk. 5:9).

Presence gives us a divinizing taste of eternal life. Presence is the elixir for all that ails us. When we drink of this 'living water,' we know intuitively we will 'never die' (cf. Jn. 4:10-14).

Presence is alert stillness. Presence is acutely focused yet completely relaxed. In Presence, our eyes are as soft as they are keen. In Presence, we are like watchmen who 'look for the Lord more than sentinels for daybreak' (cf. Ps. 130:6).

Presence is bereft of judgment or condemnation. In Presence, there is no accusation, judgment or condemnation. It is impossible for anyone steeped in Presence to judge, condemn or accuse another (cf. Lk. 6:37).

Presence makes forgiveness axiomatic. In Presence, it's not as if we *decide* to forgive others; rather, in Presence, we forgive others as automatically and 'necessarily'[48] as God does (cf. Isa. 49:15; Lk. 5:23-24).

Presence reveals all human achievements as by-products of God's prior benevolence. In Presence, we forgive others *as* God forgives us, i.e., as a result of, not a condition for, God's forgiveness. In Presence, the full impact of St. John's *kerygma* becomes obvious: 'It is not that we have loved God, but that God has loved us first' (cf. 1 Jn. 4:10).

There is no difference between abiding in Presence for a lifetime or entering it for the first time. The experience of Presence is always absolutely new, absolutely fresh. In Presence, it's as if we become again and again 'new creations in Christ' (cf. 2 Cor. 5:17).

Presence is the eternal Now breaking into time, rendering past and future irrelevant to the bliss of the present moment. In Presence, 'behold, all things are made new (cf. Rev. 21:5).

---

[48] Freedom and necessity are identical in God. For God to 'freely forgive' is to show God as 'necessarily' forgiving because 'God is love' (1 Jn 4:8).

Advice-giving is absent in Presence. In Presence, everyone minds their own business. At the same time, in Presence we empathize deeply with the sufferings of others. In Presence, we know that 'whatever is done to the least among us' is somehow done to God himself (cf. Mt. 25:40).

Presence is the redemption of loneliness, converting loneliness into solitude. In Presence, we are 'no longer orphans' (cf. Eph. 2:19) but know ourselves as 'adoptive children of God' (cf. Jn. 1:12; Gal. 4:5).

Presence is solicitous of everyone but solicits no one. Presence is the Good Samaritan who 'binds up our wounds' and asks nothing in return (cf. Lk. 10:34).

Presence makes us comfortable with ourselves so we can live comfortably with others. In Presence, we learn to 'love our neighbor *as* we love ourselves' (cf. Gal. 5:14).

In Presence, we are never less alone than when we are by ourselves. In Presence, we 'come apart by ourselves' (cf. Mk. 6:31) to commune with God. In Presence, we are one with Jesus who 'withdrew to the mountain alone' (cf. Jn. 6:15) to abide in prayer with his Father.

Being steeped in Presence is the opposite of being submerged in a crowd. Succumbing to peer pressure is death to those seeking to live in Presence. In Presence, we retreat with Jesus who, 'upon seeing the crowd, told his disciples to have a boat ready for him so that they would not crush him' (cf. Mk. 3:9).

Practicing Presence immunizes us against spiritual death. In Presence, we learn that 'to set the mind on the flesh is death, but to set the mind on the Spirit is life and peace' (cf. Rom. 8:6).

Presence is a space of both emptiness and fulfillment. In Presence, letting go and being filled with joy, peace, and compassion are a single mystery. Presence is the Mount of Beatitude where those who are 'poor in spirit inherit the kingdom of God' (cf. Mt. 5:3).

The experience of Presence is an abyss of ever-greater, ever-deeper levels of letting go and being filled up. In Presence, death and life are synonymous. In Presence, 'we are buried in Christ and simultaneously raised from the dead by the glory of the Father' (cf. Rom. 6:4).

Presence is the Paschal Mystery compacted into a single, indefinable nowhere point from which all being, consciousness and bliss are begotten. In Presence, our breath is taken away by the beauty and utterly fortuitous giftedness of the present moment. Pure, attentive, accepting awareness of being is bliss: *Sacchidānanda.*[49]

---

[49] See above, n. 1.

In Presence, the risen Christ manifests himself in the here and now. In Presence, with the apostle John, we exclaim: 'It is the Lord!' (cf. Jn. 21:7).

Discontent dissolves in Presence. In Presence, nothing abides but love. When we find the Lord in Presence, he 'delivers us from all our fears' (cf. Ps. 34:4).

Presence is impervious to evil and reveals rules for morality as irrelevant to God's higher power of mercy and forgiveness. In Presence, we 'count everything as loss and refuse,' discovering a righteousness rooted not in moral uprightness but in 'the faithfulness of Jesus Christ' (cf. Phil. 3:8-9).

Presence reveals the absolute priority of the love of God which 'surpasses all understanding' (cf. Eph. 3:19). In Presence, we realize that it 'is not we who have loved God but that God has loved us first' (cf. 1 Jn. 4:1).

In Presence, we feel as though we have been 'filled with all the fullness of God' (cf. Eph. 3:19). In Presence, we exclaim with St. Paul, 'It is I who lives, yet no longer I, but Christ who lives within and through me' (cf. Gal. 2:20).

Presence is an ever-expanding experience of redemption. In Presence, we advance 'from one degree of glory to another' (cf. 2 Cor. 3:18). Every instant we abide in Presence is a deeper purification and perfection of the previous one. In Presence, God is 'all in all' (cf. Eph. 1:23; 4:6).

Presence allows us to both acknowledge and accept unhappiness. In Presence, we are 'blissful even when we mourn, for we know we shall be comforted' (cf. Mt. 5:4).

Presence envelops unhappiness in its arms and allows it to cry itself to sleep. Even were it possible for a 'mother to forget her child,' Presence will never fail to calm our fears and give us hope (cf. Mt. 5:4).

Presence turns fear of abandonment into the abandonment of fear (cf. 1 Jn. 4:18). In Presence, we 'cast our burdens on the Lord' and find that 'he will sustain us' (Ps. 55:22). In Presence, we walk on the choppy and wind-tossed waves without fear of sinking (cf. Mt. 14:24-31).

Presence is the answer to the world's violence. Presence takes us beyond the realm of 'an eye for an eye, a tooth for a tooth' (cf. Mt. 5:38-39). Presence defeats evil, not by opposing it but by obviating it. Presence is Christ in the midst of his enemies, 'affording them no answer' such that, stopping them in their tracks, they 'wondered greatly' (cf. Mt. 27:12-14; Jn. 2:24; Mk. 11:33).

Imagine a mad man punching the air. Presence is the life-giving air, the man, humanity punching itself out. In Presence, Christ asks the world, 'How long will you harbor such evil thoughts within you?' (cf. Mt. 9:4; Jer. 4:14), 'How long will you hide your face from me? (cf. Ps. 13:1).

Presence is the promised land in which God provides for those who enter its arid emptiness (cf. Num. 20:4). In Presence, God sends ravens to feed the inspiration of prophets (cf. 1 Kg. 17:4), and manna and living water to those who seek him in faith (cf. Ex. 16:35; 1 Kg. 18:4).

Presence is a space of absolute immediacy, a world in which God gives nothing and gives everything only and exactly as it is needed. In Presence, we live like the poor 'widow of Zarephath' who, trusting God with her life, found that her 'jar of meal was never spent, neither did the pitcher of oil ever fail, according to the word of the Lord which he spoke by Elijah (cf. 1 Kg. 17:16).

In Presence, we hear God saying, 'Why do you spend your money for that which is not bread, and your labor for that which does not satisfy?' (cf. Isa. 55:2). In Presence, we take our place at the 'heavenly banquet' (cf. Rev. 19:9), enjoying a proleptic taste of the 'rich foods and choice wines' reserved for those who ascend this holy 'mountain of the Lord' (cf. Isa. 25:6).

Presence works like epsom salts - it draws out the soreness of being hurtfully human. Presence is 'the balm of Gilead' (cf. Jer. 8:22; 46:11), 'the oil and wine' of the Good Samaritan (cf. Lk. 10:33ff.) with which the Good Shepherd 'heals the brokenhearted, and binds up their wounds' (cf. Ps. 147:3).

Presence keeps 'otherness' from becoming alienation and difference from being destructive. Presence prevents alterity from becoming alienation and individuality from isolation. Presence affords us a glimpse of Jesus' promise that will we be in communion with one another as he is with the Father (cf. Jn. 7:21).

Presence is a dynamic space of perpetually transcending immanence. In Presence, we ascend to heaven and become more firmly anchored in the present. In Presence, the *Plērōma* is unveiled as a horizon of light dispelling the darkness of history. Presence is an experience of the Christ 'the same today, yesterday and forever' (cf. Heb. 13:18).

The experience of Presence is continual bliss. Stepping outside of Presence into unconscious anxiety is the very definition of hell. Yet, even hell is subversive of itself, since all suffering eventually yields to surrender. For was it not 'for the sake of the joy that lay ahead of him' that Jesus 'endured the cross, making light of its disgrace, and taking his seat at the right hand of the throne of God' (cf. Heb. 12:2)?

It's impossible to travel to the depths of hell without discovering the entrance to heaven. Once the 'outer darkness' (cf. Mt. 8:12) of our thinking has reached its breaking point, the light of hope and promise of deliverance arise. In Presence, 'My God, my God, why have you abandoned me' (cf. Mt. 27:46) gives way to 'Into your hands I commit my spirit' (cf. Lk. 23:46).

Presence is utterly disarming in its simplicity. Presence is sharing in the simplicity and compassionate aseity of God. In Presence, it's as if 'the Lamb has opened the seventh seal' and we experience 'silence in heaven for about half an hour' (cf. Rev. 8:1).

Presence is a fullness of actuality that can be neither threatened nor destroyed. In Presence, we are rendered as mute as the Pharisees who were unable 'to answer Jesus a word, nor dared to ask him any more questions' (cf. Mt. 22:46).

Presence is the invisible port available in every storm, the elusive refuge in every crisis. In Presence, like the disciples in the boat with Jesus after he calmed the storm, we are 'immediately at the land to which we are going' (cf. Jn. 6:21).

Presence is the *pause* in the harangue, the *gap* between our thoughts. Presence is discovered in the stillness that settles in after the chaos has calmed. In Presence, we are like the demoniacs who seemed to be dead (cf. Mk. 9:26) but are 'sitting there clothed and in their right minds' (cf. Mk. 5:15).

Presence conveys the love of God, even to those who don't believe in God. Neither a rant against God nor the praise of God speaks as truly about God as does simply being present. In Presence, we are always surprised by joy.[50]

---

[50] A phrase taken from C.S. Lewis' story of his conversion, *Surprised by Joy*.

God is as undeniable as the mystery of Presence, for in denying either God or presence, one presumes upon them. Those who contest the reality of God or Presence must be forgiven 'for they do not know what they are doing' (cf. Lk. 23:34).

There are many who have not yet discovered how to be knowingly present, who have not yet discovered the power of Presence. 'Many are called' to experience God in Presence, but 'few are chosen' to do so (cf. Mt. 22:14).

The hell of atheism exists only until the the heavenly bliss of Presence is experienced.

Despair is a desperate grasp for the power of Presence. In the cry of despair we can detect the prayer, 'I do believe, help thou my unbelief!' (cf. Mk. 9:24).

We never possess Presence, Presence possesses us. In Presence 'we live and move and have our being' (cf. Acts 17:28). In Presence, we realize that 'God is at work in us, both to will and to work for his good pleasure' (cf. Php. 2:13).

Presence always arises within us as pure gift. Our desire to 'be present' is itself the power of Presence awakening us to a gift that is forever ours. In Presence, our perpetual expression is, 'Lord, it is good for us to be here!' (cf. Mk. 9:5).

Presence reveals itself as the benevolent overseer of our thinking self. Presence, as it were, smiles at us when we become lost in our thoughts. Presence reminds us 'My thoughts are not your thoughts, nor your ways mine' (cf. Isa. 55:8).

Awakening to the egoic silliness of our mental busyness, we experience Presence. This awakening always has something light-hearted about it, like a loving grandparent smiling, with soft eyes, at a grandchild frustrated with their efforts to achieve (cf. Sir. 21:20).

Presence is Jesus saying to Martha - and to us - 'You have chosen the better part and it shall not be taken from you' (cf. Lk. 10:42).

Presence is the source of true relaxation. Being present is a letting go that goes all the way down. In Presence, we hear Christ saying, 'Come away and rest for a while' (cf. Mk. 6:31). In Presence, we 'enter into his rest' (cf. Mt. 11:29; Heb. 3:18).

When we void ourselves of ideas and expectations, our emptiness becomes a fullness of love, into which any evil can be placed and redeemed. Presence is a 'consuming fire' (cf. Dt. 4:24; Heb. 12:29) in which every one of our evil, empty works 'are burned up' that 'we may be saved' (cf. 1 Cor. 3:15).

Evil - such as it 'is'[51] - has no access to our hearts, where Presence arises, only to our heads. True, evil actions 'spring from the heart' (cf. Mt. 15:18; Lk. 6:45), but not before they begin first as thoughts in our minds. Presence is 'the cherubim with a flaming sword which turns every way, to guard the way to this precious tree of life' (cf. Gen. 3:24).

Presence is the sophiological locus where that which is of God (divinity) is given to that which is of not-God (humanity). Presence is the trysting point where we heart-sick humans find the love we seek (cf. Song 2:5; 3:4). Presence is the 'enclosed garden' and 'sealed fountain' (cf. Song 4:12; 6:3) where our communion with God is consummated.

Presence is the womb of divine wisdom. In Presence, we swim in the amniotic fluid of Holy *Sophia*. In Presence, we are reborn and become children fit for the 'kingdom of God' (cf. Mt. 18:3).

Presence is a profoundly prophetic space. Abiding in Presence, truth comes from us with a clarity and a convincingness otherwise impossible. In Presence, we speak and act 'with authority, not as those who speak and act in ego' (cf. Mt. 7:29).

---

[51] Evil, so-called, has no substantial reality. As the tradition holds (see St. Thomas Aquinas, *Summa Theologica*, Part 1, *Question* 5), evil is always a *privation* of the good, a *lack* of an excellence. 'Privations' and 'lacks', despite our frequent reification of them, do not exist. Or, if one prefers, they have the same 'reality' as a magician's sleight of hand. A magician's deception, though we know it has no foundation in truth, nevertheless has the *appearance* of something actual, and so is mistaken, at least momentarily, as 'real'. Therefore it is a 'deception'. So also with 'evil' - every 'sin' stems, at least in part, from deception, thus prompting Jesus to say of all so-called 'sinners', 'Father, forgive them, they do not *know* what they are doing' (cf. Lk. 23:34; cf. Jn. 8:32).

Presence is either the great uniter or the great divider. Relationships are either divinized or destroyed when one of the parties begins to live mindfully in Presence. 'Blessed are they who find no stumbling block' in Presence (cf. Lk. 7:23; 1 Cor 1:23).

Presence is a healing balm to those who discover it, and an indictment to those who do not. Abiding in Presence, we provoke judgment (cf. Jn. 9:39) while 'judging no one' (cf. Jn. 8:15-16). In Presence, we elicit condemnation but condemn no one (cf. Jn. 8:11). For 'what fellowship has the light' of Presence 'with the darkness' of the false self? (cf. 2 Cor. 6:14).

One who has tasted Presence can never go back to the way things used to be. Entering Presence means leaving the land of slavery, i.e., 'slavery to sin' (cf. Heb. 2:15) and the 'fleshpots of Egypt' (cf. Ex. 16:3), and entering the arid but fruitful 'land of milk and honey' (Ex. 33:3).

Presence reveals gentleness as the essence of who we are. Immersed in Presence, we acquire the humility of servants (cf. Mk. 10:45; Lk. 17:10) and the self-possession of kings (cf. Jn. 19:14). In Presence, we receive the 'humble and contrite heart' for which David prayed (cf. Ps. 51:17), and the power 'to do all things' of which St. Paul could boast (cf. Php. 4:13).

The desert exercises a visceral attraction upon those who practice Presence. Presence enkindles within us a burning desire to be 'alone with the Alone'. In Presence, we find solitude to be 'more precious than jewels,' and that 'nothing we desire can compare with her' (cf. Prv. 3:15).

Presence gives us faith and hope impossible to achieve on our own. Presence affords us a taste of God's unconditional love. In Presence, we know that 'even if a mother were to forget her child,' Presence will not abandon us (cf. Isa. 49:15).

'If we ascend to the heavens', Presence is there, and 'if we lie down in Sheol', Presence is there (Ps. 139:8). There is nowhere we can go where finding Presence is not 'immediately arriving at the farthest shore' of divine love (cf. Jn. 6:21).

Presence is a space of blessed impoverishment. In Presence, bereft of thoughts or agendas, we are made wealthy with an openness and compassion surpassing every created good. Presence is the 'poverty of spirit' (cf. Mt. 5:3; Prv. 16:19) that 'is more precious than gold or silver' (cf. Ps. 119:72; Prv. 22:1).

In Presence, we discover that our inner poverty is a participation in God's self-diffusive richness. In Presence, we enter into the joy of Christ who, 'though he was in the form of God, did not deem equality with God something to be possessed' (cf. Php. 2:6-11).

Presence is a share in the infinite nothingness of God. God is no-thing, a non-subsistent Mystery of self-sufficient actuality. Presence is the sophianic self-communication of God, making us icons of His own ineffable actuality. Nothing in ourselves (cf. Ps. 144:3), we are everything in God (cf. Php. 4:13) and God is everything in us (cf. Eph. 1:23; 1 Cor. 15:28).

Presence renders us relatively indifferent to the opinions of others. In Presence, criticism has little power to tear us down, nor praise to build us up. In Presence, we simply 'shake off the dust on our feet' (cf. Lk. 9:5) and keep moving towards the kingdom of God.

The prophetic power of Presence is such that it inures us to outside commentary, while making us alive to the needs of others. In Presence, we never 'throw our pearls before swine' (cf. Mt. 7:6) yet respond joyfully to the needs of 'the least of these' (cf. Mt. 25:40).

Presence is a proleptic participation in the final *telos* (purpose) and *Plērōma* (fullness) of creation. In Presence, we ecstatically anticipate the full flowering of the seeds of divinity implanted within us. In Presence, we realize that 'eye has not seen, nor ears heard, what God has prepared' for those God has created for himself (cf. 1 Cor. 2:9).

Presence is a theophanic vision which, far from generating grandiosity, engenders the deepest humility and gratitude. In Presence, even the most seemingly insignificant things are experienced as bathed in the light of eternity. In Presence, even the smallest sparrow or tiniest flower appears as a sacrament of God's creative love (cf. Mt. 10:29).

Like an electrical transformer converts overwhelming wattage into a register compatible with our appliances, Presence modulates the Source of divine Actuality (God) into a frequency that allows us to attune ourselves to it. Presence allows us 'to see the face of God and live' (cf. Ex. 33:10-11).

Presence is the governor of God's infinite creative energy that enables us to enter it, not for our destruction, but for our deification. In Presence, God 'changes our lowly body to be like his glorious body, by the power which enables him to subject all things to himself' (cf. Php. 3:20–21).

Presence is the sophianic medium that makes possible the blissful self-communication of God. Presence is a mystical ethos in which we experience the power of God without dissolution or destruction (cf. Ex. 33:20).

Presence is the filter through which God gives us a share in His divinity. Presence is the transcendent magnet which draws us to himself. In Presence, a 'wondrous exchange'[52] transpires in which all that God has is given to us, and all that we are is assimilated into the life of God (cf. Jn. 12:32; 14:26; 15:15).

Presence is the risen Christ bringing to completion the deification of humanity and the Holy Spirit 'leading us into all truth,' both about ourselves and about God (cf. Jn. 16:13).

In Presence, we are saturated with the divinity of the Holy Spirit. In Presence, our souls are like the linen cloths in the hands of Lydia, the 'dyer of purple goods' (cf. Acts 16:14). In Presence, we are 'enpurpuled' with the royal dignity of the 'King of kings' (cf. Rev. 19:16).

---

[52] The *Admirabile Commercium* is a theological way of describing the Incarnation, i.e., the inner connection between divine condescension in the descent of the Son of God from eternal glory, and the divinization of fallen man in the mystery of *theosis*.

Presence is the pneumatic tube through which God draws us up to Himself. Presence is an anagogical power lifting us far above ourselves. In Presence, we are, as it were, 'born from above' (cf. Jn. 3:7).

Presence is the 'precious oil' that softens, loosens and glistens the spirits of those who discover its saving power. Presence is like the 'aromatic nard' poured upon Jesus' head (cf. Jn. 12:3), the unctuous ointment 'running down the beard of Aaron' (cf. Ps. 133:2), and the medicinal balm applied to the sick (cf. Lk. 10:34). Presence anoints our minds, bodies and souls with the healing grace of God.

The longer we abide in Presence the happier we become. Presence rejoices everything it touches. In Presence, our awareness of the gift of being is bliss (*Sacchidānanda*). It's as if 'the stones themselves cry for joy' when we walk the road of Presence (cf. Lk. 19:40).

Presence is the bottomless, undisturbed pond which engulfs and quiets all that is dropped into it. Presence is as unlimited and unassuming as it is calm and deep. In Presence, we 'know as we are know' (cf. 1 Cor. 13:12).

It's the power of Presence that touches the hearts of the listener, not the content of the words. Words, when meaningful, serve as sacraments of Presence, not simply as instruments of communication. Listening to those who speak in Presence, we say to ourselves: 'Were not our hearts burning within us' as they explained things to us (cf. Lk. 24:32)?

Presence begins with the smallest act of letting go and widens into an ocean of fathomless depth. We can never make an end of diving into the infinite depths of Presence for the 'pearl of great price' (cf. Mt. 13:46).

Presence is infinitely unassuming. Like the Son of Man himself, Presence 'has no form to attract us' and no external 'beauty that we should desire' it' (cf. Isa. 53:2). Yet, it is in Presence that 'our transgressions are forgiven' and 'the wounds from our iniquities are healed' (cf. Isaiah 53:5).

In Presence, we discover that when we let go we are lifted up, when we surrender we are saved. In Presence we find that 'when we forgive we are forgiven' (cf. Mt. 6:12) and when 'we give it will be given to us, good measure, pressed down, shaken together, running over, poured into our laps' (cf. Lk. 6:38).

Presence is the opposite of, and the antidote to, our possessiveness. Covetousness - the root of all evil - evaporates in Presence. It is impossible to abide in Presence and continue to covet 'our neighbor's house, our neighbor's wife, or anything else that is our neighbor's' (cf. Ex. 20:17).

Presence is simultaneously a miracle of self-dispassion and self-actualization. In Presence, the sinful self disappears and the innocent inner child shows its face. In Presence, we become the 'little ones of the Lord' whose 'angels in heaven always behold the face of God' (cf. Mt.18:10).

Soft eyes is a sure sign that we are abiding in Presence. As it says of Jesus, fully present to the rich young man: 'he looked at him and loved him' (cf. Mk. 10:21).

Presence is as elusive and immediate as God's Spirit itself. Presence can be neither thought nor grasped, yet offers itself continually to our minds and hearts. To enter Presence, we must become like the blinded Saul who, 'led by the hand' to a place where 'something like scales' fall from his eyes, he 'regained his sight and was filled with the Holy Spirit' (cf. Acts 9:8, 17–18).

There is no connection between cognition and Presence. We can't think our way into Presence. What is called for here is not more effort but greater trust, not more works but greater faith (cf. Gal. 2:16; Rom. 3:27-28).

Presence is experienced anew every time it is discovered. In Presence, we are 'born again' (cf. 1 Pt. 23) as 'children of light' (cf. Eph. 5:8).

Presence is the greatest gift we can give. Presence is what makes our actions sacramental, not just exercises in sentimentality. Without Presence, politeness becomes platitudinous. In Presence, even our 'No' communicates compassion (cf. Mt. 5:37).

In Presence, it is impossible to speak ill of another. Gossip, criticism, blame and shame are transcended Presence. Presence renders us incapable of 'throwing the first stone' (cf. Jn. 8:7).

Presence is a space of perfect peace. Presence accepts everything while rejecting nothing. Presence is the Spirit of Christ saying: 'I will reject no one who comes to me' (cf. Jn. 6:37)

Presence reveals evil as our impulse to define something or someone as evil. Thinking indicts, Presence redeems. Presence forbids us from labeling anything as 'good' or 'evil,' for 'no one is good but God alone' (cf. Lk. 18:1).

Presence transmutes anger into grief, irritation into empathy. Presence allows us to view the character defects of ourselves and others more with compassion than consternation. Presence teaches us that it is 'mercy not sacrifice' that God desires (cf. Hos. 6:6; Mt. i9:13; 12:7).

Presence takes the edge off impatience. Presence tones down perfectionism. Presence compels us to adopt the posture of the publican: 'God, be merciful to me, a sinner!' (cf. Lk. 18:13).

Presence is God's dramamine for our seasick psyches. In Presence, we are not tempted to throw anyone overboard (cf. Jon. 1:15) because we are 'afraid of the wind and the waves' of our turbulent world (cf. Mt. 14:30).

Presence shows us that God's timing is always perfect. Nothing happens in Presence that is not given in the present moment, just as we need it, just when we need it. Presence is our 'guiding star' to discover where salvation lies (cf. Mt. 2:7-10).

Every foreground has a background. Every object is situated within a wider horizon. Presence is the unthematic Background of all possible backgrounds, the transcendent Horizon of all conceivable horizons. No matter how far into Presence we advance, the mystery of Presence forever exceeds our grasp (cf. 1 Kg. 8:27; Ps. 96:4).

Presence is as ungraspable as God to whom it connects us. In Presence, we know the One 'who alone has immortality and dwells in unapproachable light, whom no man has ever seen or can see' (1 Tim. 6:16).

The more Presence summons us forward, the further it exceeds our reach. The further Presence eludes our grasp, the more fully we desire it. 'Our hearts are restless until they rest in Presence'.[53]

In Presence, everything is shown, never told. In Presence, Wisdom arises unexpectedly as a gift and shimmers as revelation, exhibiting a certain kerygmatic power. We stand mute with the manifestation of Presence (cf. Mk. 9:6).

Presence reveals human nature to be that of *homo adorans,* not *homo sapien* or *homo faber.* In Presence, we realize our human dignity as 'a chosen race, a royal priesthood, a holy nation, God's own people, that we may declare the wonderful deeds of him who called you out of darkness into his marvelous light' (cf. 1 Pt. 2:9).

---

[53] As St. Augustine famously states: 'Our hearts are restless until they rest in you, O God' (*Confessions*, I, 1-2).

In Presence, everything is epiphanic. Awakening to wisdom in Presence is being illumined by a series of anagogical eruptions. In Presence, light, love, joy and peace erupt within us as 'a fountain of living water' (cf. Jer. 2:13; Song 4:15; Jn. 4:14; 7:38), making our lives blossom like a 'tree of life for the healing of the nations' (cf. Rev. 22:2).

To write or speak about Presence is fruitless unless every word flows directly from Presence. In Presence, we are infused with a kind of ancient-yet-ever-new wisdom that comes from God. In Presence, we become 'scribes trained for the kingdom of heaven,' knowing how to bring out of our treasure what is new and what is old' for 'the life of the world' (cf. Mt. 13:52; Jn. 6:33).

Presence is the cure for intellectual pride. That which is shown in Presence inspires praise and dissolves pretense. In Presence, we wait for direction to arise; otherwise, we are 'blind guides leading the blind falling into a pit of darkness together' (cf. Mt. 15:14).

In Presence, we develop a kind of spiritual Alzheimer's. In Presence, memories of our past accomplishments, as well as our misdeeds, fade away. We are struck blind with the uncreated light of God. Like Saul on the road to Damascus (cf. Acts 9:1ff.), or the blind man at the pool of Siloam (cf. Jn. 9:1ff.), we enter a luminous darkness 'that God may be glorified' in us (cf. Jn. 11:4).

Stay in your head too long and you'll find mendacity and malice. Abide in Presence for a single moment, and you'll experience everlasting mirth and mercy (cf. Ps. 100:5).

There is no other guru or spiritual guide than Presence. Anyone we call our teacher is taught by being present. 'Call no one your teacher, for you have but one teacher' - Presence (cf. Mt. 23:8).

Teachers are purveyors of wisdom only to the degree they are possessed of Presence. This is why Christ, the Self-presencing of God, says: 'I have not spoken on my own authority; the Father who sent me has himself commanded me what to say and what to speak' (cf. Jn. 12:49)

Presence operates in true spiritual guides like music in a virtuoso: it plays them, they don't play it. As the poet, Hafiz, says, 'I am a hole in the flute that the Christ's breath moves through; listen to this music'. Or St. Paul insists, 'It is no longer I who live, but Christ who lives in me' (cf. Gal. 2:20).

True spiritual teachers seek emptiness of mind, just as hermits seek the empty desert. In the emptiness of self-transcending availability, the teacher is given what to say. Only 'the wisdom from above is pure, peaceable, gentle, open to reason, full of mercy, without uncertainty or insincerity' (cf. Jas. 3:17).

Presence is the virginal womb in which divine wisdom is immaculately conceived. Presence arises within us without human generation. 'That which is born of the flesh is flesh, and Presence, which is born of the Spirit, is spirit' (cf. Jn. 3:6).

Presence and self-possession arise together, as do Presence and self-dispossession. Presence is the holographic medium wherein our ego dissolves and our true identity is revealed. In Presence, 'the old passes away and the new appears' (cf. 2 Cor. 5:17).

Presence imparts both supreme confidence and utter humility. In Presence, we receive ourselves as a gift from a Source other and greater than ourselves. In Presence, we experience ourselves both as 'unworthy servants' (cf. Lk. 17:10) and 'adopted children of God' (cf. Jn. 1:12-13; Rom. 8:16; Gal. 4:5).

The moment we shift from thinking to simply noticing, 'the light from on high dawns upon us' (cf. Lk. 1:78). In Presence, we are awakened, as if from a bad dream. In Presence, like Jacob, 'we are roused from our sleep and exclaim, 'Surely the Lord is in this place and we did not know it' (cf. Gen. 28:16).

Presence is an ocean of compassion that defeats the strength of all who are drowning in thought. Presence is a wellspring of patience that outlasts those who fight against it. Presence is the fullness of non-resisting love that defeats every evil and 'puts all enemies under its feet' (cf. 1 Cor. 15:25).

Presence is the experience of self-transcendence that intimates a Reality beyond itself. Presence shows us that we carry a Power within us that is greater than ourselves. In Presence, we know 'we have this treasure in earthen vessels, to show that the transcendent power belongs to God and not to us' (cf. 2 Cor. 4:7).

We are possessed *of* Presence and possessed *by* Presence, but we are *not in possession of* Presence. Presence is at once the Source of our existence and the *Plērōma* (fullness) of who and what we are. 'Let they who boast, boast (only) of the Lord' (cf. 2 Cor. 10:17).

The fact that we can stand back from ourselves and assess ourselves reveals that our deepest identity partakes of a Presence that precedes and prompts our ability to do so. With God, Presence 'guards our coming in and going out' (cf. Ps. 121:8). With Christ, Presence proclaims, 'Before Abraham was, I am' (cf. Jn. 8:48).

Presence is a continually arresting, amazing and defining experience for those who experience it. In Presence, we 'no longer believe because of another's words, for we have seen for ourselves and know that this is indeed the Savior of the world' (cf. Jn. 4:42).

Our experience of Presence confirms the aphorism that 'we are not human beings having a spiritual experience but spiritual beings having a human experience'. In Presence, we have the distinct sense that 'before we were conceived in our mothers' wombs', we are known by and one with God (cf. Jer. 1:5; Eph. 1:4).

The fact that we can place the whole of our memories into Presence shows us that we are always very much greater than them. In Presence, we realize our true identities are revealed from the future, not determined by our past. In Presence, we 'forget what lies behind and strain forward to what lies ahead' (cf. Php. 3:13)

In Presence, we encounter a power of consciousness beyond cognition, judgment and representation. In Presence, we experience a kind of 'inverse intentionality,'[54] i.e., we 'know as we are being known' (cf. 1 Cor. 13:12), we 'see as we are being seen' (cf. 1 Jn. 3:2).

Presence is beyond dialectic and sublation, beyond dualities and polarities. Presence is the Source of whole without being a part of the whole. Presence is an energetic manifestation of the divine *Logos* in whom 'all things hold together' (cf. Col. 1:17).

Presence is the silent music of the spheres. In Presence, we are, as it were, invited to play music on a soundless piano. In Presence, 'There is no speech nor are there words, yet its voice goes out through all the earth, even to the ends of the world' (cf. Ps. 19:3–4).

---

[54] An idea borrowed from John Panteleimon Manoussakis, *God After Metaphysics: A Theological Aesthetic.* Jean-Luc Marion describes the same phenomenon as 'counter-intentionality' in his book, *In Excess: Studies of Saturated Phenomenon.*

Presence grants us the gift of eternal youth. We grow younger, never older, when abiding in Presence. Presence is the womb of our perpetual rebirth. In Presence, we are 'born anew, not of perishable seed but of that which is imperishable' (cf. 1 Pt. 1:23).

Presence is not stoicism. Presence is ecstatically personal but not egoistic. Presence is imperturbably but not indifferent. In Presence, we love intensely but we 'do not cling' to the beloved (cf. Jn. 20:17).

In Presence, we realize, with pure joy, that we will always be learners. We bow before Presence as beginners before a Zen master. In Presence, we realize we 'have but one master', God himself (cf. Mt. 23:10).

Our willingness to listen and learn, no matter the cost, brings divine bliss. Presence is a space of limitless listening. The moment 'the voice of Presence comes to our ears, our spirits leap for joy' (cf. Lk. 1:44).

We are the servants, not the masters, of Presence. Presence precedes and begets us. In Presence, we assume the posture of the Son in the Trinity, who, 'though he was in the form of God, did not deem equality with God the Father as something to be grasped at; rather, he humbled himself, taking on the form of a servant' (cf. Phil. 2:6-11).

Presence at once slakes and stimulates our insatiable thirst for the Infinite. In Presence, our souls are 'athirst for the living God' (Ps. 42:2) while we also 'drink deeply with delight from the abundance of God's living water' (cf. Isa. 66:11; 55:1; Jn. 4:11; 7:38).

Presence mutes the interpretive elements of our minds and opens us to the romance of seeking God in all things. Presence is the answer to our question, 'Have you seen him whom my soul loves?' (cf. Song 3:3).

Presence moves us beyond dialectics, divisions and debates. It elevates us above polarities, paradoxes and opposites. Presence is the Mystery *non aliud*: so completely 'other' as to be 'other than anything other'. Abiding in Presence, 'our adversaries are put to shame and those who see us rejoice at the glorious things that are done' (cf. Lk. 13:17).

Presence is not in competition with anything but illumines the beauty of everything. To those abiding in Presence, 'all things are pure'. Apart from Presence, 'nothing is pure, and our minds and consciences are corrupted' (cf. Ti. 1:15).

Abiding in Presence can be compared with no other action, yet everything we do is incomparably better done in Presence. In Presence, even 'giving a cup of cold water' is a work of divine worth (cf. Mt. 10:42).

Presence replaces gossip with gratitude, resentment with a desire to reconcile. In Presence, we receive the awareness and aptitude 'to be reconciled with others' before approaching God (cf. 2 Cor. 5:20). In Presence, we know that it is mercy, not mendacity, that God desires (cf. Hos. 6:6).

Presence is so teleologically beautiful, so anagogically blissful that it renders those divinized by it incapable of seeing, hearing or doing evil. Anyone enlivened by Presence 'does not commit sin, for God's seed abides in him' (cf. 1 Jn. 3:9).

To compare is to despair. In Presence, we bask in the light of the eternal Now where comparison, complaining, criticizing and condemning are non-existent. In Presence, we find only 'love, joy, peace, patience, kindness, goodness, faithfulness, gentleness, self-control. Against such there is no law' (cf. Gal. 5:22–23).

Presence cannot be reduced to a discreet act of intentional awareness. Even sadists and sociopaths exhibit intentional awareness in their acts of malevolence. Presence is a mystery of self-transcendence such that, in Presence, we are prevented from doing deliberate or intentional harm. In Presence, 'we cannot sin because we are born of God' (cf. 1 Jn. 3:9).

In Presence, we know ourselves as begotten by God, just as Christ is the only-begotten Son (cf. Jn. 3:16-16; 1 Jn. 5:1; Acts 13:33). In Presence, we become by participation what Christ is by nature. In Presence, 'If we live, we live to the Lord, and if we die, we die to the Lord; so, whether we live or whether we die, we are one with the Lord' (cf. Rom. 14:8).

Presence affords us a *Sapientia* superior to, but not in opposition to, analytical thinking. In Presence, we know that we know nothing; yet, we also know we are in possession of 'wisdom and understanding beyond measure' (cf. Ps. 147:5; 1 Kg. 4:19; Col. 1:9).

In Presence, we know ourselves as 'unworthy servants' (cf. Lk. 17:10). Presence is a gift, the gift that never stops giving. For what, in Presence, 'do we have that we did not receive? If then we received it, why would we ever boast as if it were not a gift?' (cf. 1 Cor. 4:7).

Our voraciousness for Presence is matched only by our gratitude to experience it. Presence is the end of greediness and the 'fulfillment of all our desires' (cf. Ps. 20:4).

Presence unmasks pride, self-hatred and despair, not as evil, but as petty. Presence shows temper tantrums to be so many tempests in a teapot. Presence promises that the 'fires of Gehenna' will eventually burn themselves out (cf. Mk. 9:43).

Presence is the uncapturable, tacit dimension of our existence. Presence is the uncreated Light in which we see all other lights (cf. Ps. 36:9). As Meister Eckhart observed long ago: 'The eye through which we see God is the same eye through which God sees us; our eye and God's eye are one eye, one seeing, one knowing, one love'.[55]

---

[55] Sermon IV, *'True Hearing'*. See: http://www.ccel.org/ccel/eckhart/sermons.vii.html.

When we attempt to make Presence an object of our focal attention, it eludes us. When we try to live knowingly in Presence, it escapes our grasp. Presence is the unthematic and unreachable horizon in which 'we live and move and have our being' (cf. Acts 17:28).

We cannot grasp Presence any more than we can catch our shadow. We cannot possess Presence any more that we can see our eyes. We cannot touch Presence any more than we can touch the tip of our finger with the same finger. Presence 'goes before us, giving us the treasures of darkness in secret places, that we may know the Lord, who calls us by name' (cf. Isa. 45:2–3).

To say we can never separate ourselves from Presence is saying far too little. There is nothing, 'neither death, nor life, nor things present, nor things to come, nor height, nor depth, nor anything else in all creation', which, if seen in the light of Presence, does not reveal itself as the love of God (cf. Rom. 8:38-39).

Before we are this or that, *we are. That* we are is infinitely more important - and more arresting - than *what* we are. In Presence, we share in God's Wisdom, showing us that, even 'before the foundation of the world' (cf. Eph. 1:4), we are God's 'daily delight' because God 'rejoices in his inhabited world and delights in the sons of men' (cf. Prv. 8:30–31).

Awareness of our 'I-am-ness' is the closest we can get to knowing ourselves as God knows us 'before we were conceived in our mother's womb' (cf. Jer. 1:5; Job 31:151-18; Lk. 2:21). Presence affords us a sneak peek into our lives that 'are hidden with Christ in God' (cf. Col. 3:3). One such peek makes the rest of our perceptions of self and others seem like self-hypnosis.

Presence is not passivity. Presence is a space of alert attentiveness without agenda. In Presence, we remain silent and compassionate, allowing others 'to throw the first stone' (cf. Jn. 8:7).

Presence is an experience of transcendental openness to we-know-not-what. Yet, this 'know-not-what' of our transcendental orientation is the Source and fulfillment of its teleological aim. Presence is the 'Alpha and Omega' (cf. Rev. 1:8) of our desire for God.

Presence is the opposite of stoic detachment or oriental indifference. In Presence, we intentionally relax into the embrace of the present moment. In Presence, we find enlivening restfulness which our weary spirits seek (cf. Ps. 23:2; 116:7; Mt. 11:29).

Presence is a letting go that is simultaneously an opening up. Presence is a deliberate relinquishment of expectations in anticipation of transcendental peace. There is nothing we surrender in Presence that we don't 'receive a hundredfold in return' (cf. Mk. 10:30).

Presence is infinitely creative. Devoid of intellection, Presence generates intuitive ingenuity, creative genius. In Presence, we receive a wisdom that 'confounds our adversaries' (cf. Ps. 44:7). In Presence, we 'hear new things, hidden things which we have not known' (cf. Isa. 48:6).

In Presence, we intuit 'the plan of the mystery hidden for ages in God who created all things' (cf. Eph. 3:9). In Presence, we are given to glimpse 'what has been hidden since the foundation of the world' (cf. Mt. 13:35).

We abide in Presence always as its servant, never its owner. We abide in Presence as Jesus abided in his Father, 'never deeming equality with God something to be grasped or possessed' (cf. Phil. 2:6-11). Presence is a participation in the humility of the *Logos* who 'came to serve, not be served' (cf. Mk. 10:45).

Presence is a wellspring of 'living water that bubbles up within us' (cf. Jn. 4:14) from an inexhaustible Source beyond ourselves. Presence flows through us like the 'river of life,' making us fruitful 'for the healing of the nations' (cf. Rev. 22:1-5).

Presence shines within us as a light that never goes out. Even when it diminishes like a 'smoldering wick, it is never extinguished' (cf. Isa. 42:3; Mt. 12:20). Presence is a proleptic participation in the heavenly Jerusalem where 'night shall be no more and where neither light nor lamp is needed, for the Lord God will be our light, and we shall reign with God for ever and ever' (cf. Rev.22:1–5).

Presence engenders a fierce yet humble fidelity. Once discovered, we 'give all we have' (cf. Mt. 13:44) to abide in Presence. In Presence, we say, like Ruth, 'where you go I will go, and where you lodge I will lodge' (cf. Ruth 1:16).

Fidelity to Presence can overcome infidelity in any relationship. Presence is a participation in the 'faithfulness of Christ' (cf. Gal. 2:16) [*pistis Christou*],[56] which allowed Jesus to forgive the sins of the world (cf. 1 Jn. 2:2), and to exhort his followers to forgive 'not seven times, but seventy-seven times' (cf. Mt. 18:22).

Ignorance or forgetfulness of Presence is the root cause of the world's evil. Sin is the unconscious default position of those who 'are darkened in their understanding, alienated from the life of God because of the ignorance that is in them' (Eph. 4:18). Hence, Jesus' words on the Cross: 'Father, forgive them, they *know not* what they do' (cf. Lk. 23:34).

Apart from Presence, 'it is impossible to please God' (cf. Heb. 11:6). Outside of Presence, we are deaf, dumb and blind, fully lacking in situational awareness (cf. Isa. 42:8; Mt. 15:30). Without Presence, 'we know how to interpret the appearance of the sky, but we cannot interpret the signs of the times'.(cf. Mt. 16:3).

---

[56] The ultimate meaning of 'salvation' is 'participation in the *pistis Christou*,' i.e., in 'the faithfulness of Jesus to His Father'. Adopting a *participative* approach to our life 'in Christ,' as well as contemplating the '*faithfulness of Christ*' vis-a-vis His Father, are the keys to understanding salvation as *theosis*, i.e., as deification (cf. 2 Pt. 1:4). For an extended discussion of this 'participative' approach to salvation 'in the *faithfulness of* Christ' and its implications for a New Perspective on St. Paul, see N. T. Wright, *Pauline Perspectives: Essays on Paul*.

Knowledge without wisdom is stupidity, perception without Presence is darkness. Only the transcendent light of Presence can expel the darkness that envelops the 'world of the flesh' (cf. Jn. 3:66; 1 Jn. 2:16; Gal. 5:16-17). Failing Presence, 'the suns and the moons of our internal geography are darkened, and our guiding stars withdraw their shining' (cf. Joel 3:15).

Principles do not have the power of Presence. Principles appeal to the head, Presence to the heart. Those who conflate abiding in Presence with principled behavior 'honor God with their lips, but their hearts are far from him' (cf. Mt. 15:8).

One cannot abide in Presence and remain the least bit proud. In Presence, we see, as Mary did, that 'God scatters the proud in their conceit and lifts up the lowly' (cf. Lk. 1:51-52). Or, as Peter had to learn: 'God opposes the proud, but gives grace to the humble' (cf. 1 Pt. 5:5; cf. Mt. 16:23; Prv 3:34; Jas. 4:6).

In Presence, the social order appears as collective hubris, an arrangement of collective insanity. We are 'brought low in all the world' through our lack of Presence (cf. Dan. 3:14-15). Ours is a 'slavery to sin' (cf. Jn. 8:34), from which only the light of God's truth - Presence - can set us free (cf. Jn. 8:32; cf. Rom. 6:18).

Presence is neither abstract nor impersonal. Presence is the dissolution of the persona, not the person. In Presence, we glimpse our true, infinitely-loved identity in Christ (cf. Col. 3:3). In Presence, we learn to 'love one another as we love ourselves' (cf. Mk. 12:31), and to 'love one another as God has loved us' (cf. Jn. 13:34; 1 Jn. 4:10-12).

In Presence, our true colors do not fade but become unimaginably more radiant. In Presence, we momentarily see ourselves as God sees us (cf. 1 Cor. 13:12) and are 'surprised by joy'.[57] Beholding our true colors, however briefly, in Presence, Jesus' desire is fulfilled, i.e., that his 'joy may be in us, and that our joy may be complete' (cf. Jn. 15:11).

Presence is the opposite of unconscious conformism. Presence engenders an active resistance to peer pressure. Presence will not allow us to surrender to mindless routine. Instead, Presence imbues us with 'the mind of Christ' (cf. 1 Cor. 2:16) who 'makes all things new' (cf. Rev. 21:5).

Presence is God's cure for spiritual sclerosis. Before encountering Presence, we are like the paralyzed 'man at the pool of Bethesda who had been ill for thirty-eight years'. In Presence, we hear Christ's words: 'Rise, take up your pallet, and walk'. At once we are healed. We rise and walk with the 'freedom of the children of God' (cf. John 5:5–9; Rom. 8:21).

In Presence, we can speak without needing words. Speaking without Presence - whether inveighing, invoking, exhorting or whatever - we sound like 'a noisy gong or a clanging cymbal' (cf. 1 Cor. 13:1). Presence is the Spirit enlivening the living Word to be the voice and face of the Father (cf. Jn. 14:9).

---

[57] Taken from the title of C. S. Lewis' spiritual autobiography, *Surprised by Joy*.

Presence is the mysterious space of self-transcendence. Presence is the *diastasis* ('distance')[58] within ourselves, and from ourselves, where we discover our true, God-given selves. Presence is what allows Jesus to say, without contradiction, 'the Father and I are one' (cf. Jn. 10:30) and 'the Father is greater than I' (cf. Jn. 14:28).

Embroiled in thinking, we have many questions but no definitive answers. In Presence, there are no questions. In Presence, we 'ask no more questions' of God (cf. Lk. 20:40), trusting fully that God has only to 'say the word and we shall be healed' (cf. Lk. 7:7).

In Presence, we can hear 'the sound of one hand clapping'.[59] Like the parables of Christ, the purpose of a koan is to point us to Presence. Presence is the Way - the Tao - to discover Christ as the Truth and Life of the world (cf. Jn. 14:6).

---

[58] Hans Urs von Balthasar believes that a certain 'distance' or 'separation' (*diastasis*) is revealed in the Trinity as a divine form of union. Quoting Adrienne von Speyr, he says, 'During the Passion the Spirit maintains the internal divine *diastasis* between Father and Son in its economic form, so that what seems to us to be the sign of separation of Father and Son is precisely the sign of greatest unification....The separation that is perceptible to us is the highest proof of definitive unity, for if they had not been so certain of their unity, they would not have been able to go as far as the mystery of the night of the Cross without producing alienation, misunderstanding or the division of truth'. See Hans Urs von Balthasar, *Theo-Drama: Theological Dramatic Theory, volume V: The Last Act*, p. 262, quoting Adrienne Von Speyr, *The Gospel of John: The Farewell Discourses: Meditations on John 13-17*, p. 358.
[59] Classical Zen Koan.

Presence unveils a world beyond our problems. Presence reminds us that prior to understanding there is astonishment at being. In Presence, we are arrested by the mystery of the great I AM (Ex. 3:14) saying, 'Let it be!' (cf. Gen. 1:3).

Presence beholds the beauty even of that which seems off kilter. Presence bathes everything in a *penumbra* of divine radiance. It is not sin that accounts for the world's blindness but 'that the glory of God may be manifested' in its darkness (cf. Jn. 9:3; 11:4).

In Presence, we acquire the emotional equivalent of a safecracker's touch. In Presence, we learn how to handle things so gently that they open of their own accord. Touched by Presence, 'our eyes are opened and we glorify God' (cf. Mt. 9:8, 30).

Practicing Presence inspires an incitement to create. Presence is a participation in the on-going creativity of God. In Presence, we 'will also do the works that Christ does, and even greater works than these will we do' (cf. Jn. 14:12).

Presence engenders a quiet but fierce fidelity in those possessed of it. Presence exerts an allure, an invitation to a hidden tryst with God in the eternal Now. In Presence, we hear God calling: 'Arise, my love, my dove, my fair one, and come away with me' (cf. Song 2:10).

Presence generates pure gratitude. In Presence, we open ourselves, without judgment, to all that is, accepting everything as pure gift. Abiding in Presence, we wonder 'what thanksgiving we can render to God' for all the joy we feel ? (cf. 1 Th. 3:9).

Benevolence is the ineluctable ethos of Presence. In Presence, kindness comes naturally. In Presence, it is impossible not to 'do unto others as we would have them do unto us' (cf. Lk. 6:31).

Presence is the virginal space in which our nuptial communion with God is consummated. Presence is an anticipatory sharing in the 'Wedding Feast of the Lamb' (cf. Rev. 19:7). In Presence, we are 'espoused to God forever in love and mercy' (cf. Hos. 2:19-20).

Meeting another in Presence, they become, as it were, a part of us. In Presence, a kind of 'communion of saints' is constellated in which we feel ourselves to be 'one body, one spirit in Christ' (cf. 1 Cor. 12:13). As members of 'one body in Christ and individually members one of another' (cf. Rom. 12:5), 'the peace of Christ rules in our hearts,' filling us with gratitude and thanksgiving (cf. Col. 3:15).

Presence is a state of willing permeability which never becomes codependence. In Presence, we make room for the other within ourselves - even *as* ourselves - without compromising our own, primordial identity in God. In Presence, we 'rejoice with those who rejoice and weep with those who weep' (cf. Rom. 12:15), knowing that 'he who sees in secret will reward us in secret' (cf. Mt. 6:4-6).

Presence is a mystery of spiritual availability (*disponibilité*)[60] that enhances, rather than evacuates, our personal identity. In Presence, we are 'acting persons'.[61] In Presence, we allow ourselves to be 'indwelt' by the other, yet we receive the other from a center of personal self-possession. In Presence, we 'lay down our life' for the other (cf. 1 Jn. 3:16), only to 'take it up again' (cf. Jn. 10:17).

In Presence, we are at the disposal of others in a way that transcends altruism and avoids patronization. Presence is a space of mystical empathy in which 'the other and I are one,' (cf. Jn. 10:30), yet the other is never 'greater than I' (cf. Jn. 14:28).

Every form of negativity - argumentation, accusation, sarcasm, cynicism, criticism, etc. - is anathema to Presence. Yet, Presence anathematizes nothing, including negativity. In Presence, scapegoaters are not scapegoated, those who judge are not judged. Grief, yes (cf. Mk. 3:5), condemnation, no (cf. Lk. 6:37).

Presence is the space where egoic outbursts are received and dissolved. Presence is the graveyard of melodrama and histrionics. Presence is the place where God says 'Hush, hush!' to the blusterous bloviations of the world (cf. Mk. 1:25).

---

[60] For an explanation of the term '*Disponibilité*', see Hans Urs von Balthasar, *Explorations in Theology, Volume IV*, pp. 153-69.

[61] A term borrowed from the title and the content of Karol Wojtyla's book, *The Acting Person*.

Presence is always experienced as an encounter with the Infinite. In Presence, the whole of our being opens and extends outward to a Power of attraction greater than ourselves. Presence is the risen and ascended Christ 'drawing all things to himself' (cf. Jn. 12:32; 1 Cor. 15:28; Col. 1:20).

In Presence, we encounter a self-communicative mystery of infinite Generosity. In Presence, we 'reap that for which we did not labor' (cf. Jn. 4:38), and experience a gift from God that 'is not of our own doing' (cf. Eph. 2:8).

We feel intimately known in Presence. In Presence, we feel seen before we see (cf. Jer. 1:5), known before we know (cf. Eph. 1:4). In Presence, we share in the astonished delight of Nathaniel when he heard Jesus say, 'Before Philip called you, when you were under the fig tree, I saw you (cf. Jn. 1:48).

Presence is being drawn into an unnameable embrace of supra-personal Love. In Presence, we know that God knows us better than we know ourselves (cf. 1 Cor. 13:12). In Presence, we intuitively understand that it is 'not that we love God but that God loves us first' (cf. 1 Jn. 4:10-19).

Presence is is a state of intentional docility, of purposeful innocence. In Presence, we acquire a second naiveté that is wise to, but not worried about, the ways of the world. In Presence, we are 'in the world but not of it' (cf. Jn. 15:19).

Presence disposes us naturally to others, and others to us. In Presence, a 'power goes out from us' that heals those we touch (cf. Lk. 6:19; 8:46).

Those who gather at the doorway of Presence are delivered from their suffering (cf. Mk. 1:32-33). Presence is a field of accepting love that offers respite to all who enter it. In Presence, God 'makes us lie down in green pastures, leading us beside still waters until he restores our souls' (cf. Ps. 23:2–3).

Presence is what makes the difference between a saint and a social worker. Presence is what turns a counselor into a confidant, a father into a daddy (cf. Gal. 4:6).

Neither drama nor trauma find purchase in Presence, yet both serve their purpose when they awaken us to Presence. It is because we sinned that we are blinded by our histrionics, only so 'the glory of God may be made manifest through them' (cf. Jn. 9:3; 11:4).

'Duty' has no place in Presence. Presence knows nothing of 'obligation'. Presence communicates gratuity, goodness and grace; freedom, joy and gladness. Presence is a why-less love in which we 'do nothing by compulsion but with full consent and of our own free will' (cf. Phlm. 14).

Presence is an *ethos* of holy communion. Presence is automatic self-dispossession in deference to the other. In Presence, we share in the compassion of Christ who 'upon seeing the crowds, had compassion for them, because they were harassed and helpless, like sheep without a shepherd' (cf. Mt. 9:36).

Love flows like electricity as soon as we plug into Presence. Presence illumines everything in its indefinable radiance. Entering the light of Presence, we become 'the light of the world' (cf. Mt. 5:14).

Presence is never without an invisible smile, a light in the eyes, levity in the heart. Presence is joyous attentiveness, a gaze always more grateful than grave. In Presence, we acquire the vision of Christ who 'looked at the rich young man and loved him' (cf. Mk. 10:21).

Presence is an indefinable connection, often conveyed simply with a smile, a handshake, an intonation. We know it when we see it, even if its definition eludes us.

In Presence, 'heart speaks to heart' without words: *Cor ad cor loquitur*[62].

---

[62] The personal motto of John Henry Newman.

Presence is radical reciprocity, but not a 'this-for-that'. Presence is mutual space-making. Attentive, loving silence is at the heart of the self-dispossession that occurs in Presence. Presence is at once a *kenosis* and our *theosis*.

Presence is undivided, unqualified availability to the other. Such availability conquers alienation. We are alienated from others to the extent that we are not present to them. It's not possible to pretend Presence or to pretend *in* Presence. In Presence, we resemble Nathaniel 'in whom there is no guile' (cf. Jn. 1:47).

We can feign sympathy or empathy, but not Presence. When we practice Presence, genuine sympathy and empathy occur naturally. In Presence, we resemble the Good Samaritan who could not *not* attend to the the one fallen by the wayside (cf. Lk. 10:34-35).

Presence is the end of posturing and pretense. In Presence, we assume the humble position of the Publican: 'Lord, be merciful to me, a sinner' (cf. Lk. 18:13).

Presence beckons, it never commands. There is no 'supposed to' in Presence. We are not present when we tell ourselves, 'I'm supposed to be present here'. Either we are or we are not. There is no lukewarm, middle ground (cf. Rev. 13:15-16).

Presence is both the condition for and consequence of 'purity of heart' (cf. Mt. 5:8).

In Presence, we experience things exactly as they are supposed to be. Or, rather, in Presence we cannot imagine things being other than the way they are at the present moment. Judgments about 'what if' or 'why couldn't' simply do not arise. In Presence, we never question God, not as a result of being cowed by his power, but in awe of his unfathomable goodness (cf. Ps. 27:1).

In Presence, gratitude replaces misgiving as our *modus operandi*. In Presence, we ask, rhetorically: 'If God is for us, who is against us?' (cf. Rom. 8:31). In Presence, we wonder: 'Who has a god so near as the Lord our God is to us?' (Dt. 4:7). In Presence, we say: 'What thanksgiving can we render to God for all the joy which we feel?' (cf. 1 Th. 3:9).

In Presence, we see all things as beautiful, yet Presence is never pollyannaish. Presence bathes reality in God's beneficent light, but in Presence we still see the jagged edges of a violent world. In Presence, we behold all without judgment, but not without discernment (cf. Jn. 2:25; Mt. 10:16).

Critical thinking can easily become sclerosis for our souls. Presence dissolves the mental plaque that hardens our hearts (cf. Mk. 10:5).

Presence manifests the seminal mystery of the cosmos, i.e., that death and life are not antonyms but synonyms. Presence is life in death, simultaneously and seamlessly. Jesus' death and resurrection are a single event, enacted sequentially in deference to us 'foolish men and women who are slow to believe all that the prophets have spoken!' (cf. Lk. 24:25).

The death of the ego is a *result* of Presence, not an achievement prior to Presence, just as repentance is a *consequence of* forgiveness, not a condition for it. It was *because of* the 'great love she bore for him' that the sinful woman's sins had been forgiven' (cf. Lk. 7:47).

Presence fills any situation with an electric current of spiritual aliveness, but at a frequency that does not short-circuit us with its supernatural power. In Presence, we are transfigured with the soft light of divine love. When we open our spiritual eyes in Presence, 'we see only Jesus' (cf. Mt. 17:8).

That which is not assumed into Presence is not healed.[63]

Presence is God's divine tuning fork bringing us into perfect harmony with all that is. Presence attunes us to the whisperings of God's Spirit. In Presence, we 'hear things that cannot be told, things which human beings may not utter' (cf. 2 Cor. 12:4).

---

[63] Cf. Gregory of Nazianzus, *Letter 101.*

There are no problems for those who offer no resistance to the form of the present moment. Presence is permanent insulation against the raging storms of mental turmoil. In Presence, we are always 'sitting there in our right minds' (cf. Mk. 5:15).

The violence that results from the clashes of the world's polarities serves as a blessed invitation to return to Presence. In Presence, there is no evil other than not seeing the world's dichotomies for what they are. In Presence, we see clearly that God 'makes his sun rise on the evil and on the good, and sends rain on the just and on the unjust' (cf. Mt. 5:45).

Our world is the world of opposites: north-south, east-west, up-down, over-under, male-female, Democrat-Republican, etc. Presence takes us out of the world of opposites into the Unity of Being. In Presence, we discover Christ who 'holds all things together in himself' (cf. Col. 1:17).

There is no limit to how completely we can let go of our attachments. Presence invites us to enter the blessed abyss of God's own *kenosis*.[64] In Presence, we hear the call of Christ, 'Put out into the deep' (*Duc et altum*) (cf. Lk. 5:4).

Presence is the sacred space of stepping back from the world of bread and circuses and entering the 'Marriage Feast of the Lamb' (Rev. 19:9). Presence is stepping off the merry-go-round of the world's dizzying entertainment to enter the divine dance[65] of Father, Son and Holy Spirit (cf. 2 Sam. 6:14).

---

[64] See above, n.

[65] See Richard Rohr, *The Divine Dance: The Trinity and Your Transformation*.

Presence is a space of 'allowing' in which even the words of our worst enemies lose their power to harm us. Allowed to be, such words evaporate in an ocean of silent acceptance. All the evil of the world finds itself silenced in the self-possessed Presence of Jesus before Caiaphas and Pilate (cf. Mk. 15:5).

Presence dissolves the thrusts of aggression and retaliation. Presence is the antidote to the world's reciprocal violence.[66] In Presence, Christ offers a way out of our 'house of mirrors' (cf. 3 Jn. 11; Mt. 23:3).

Apart from Presence, reactivity is inevitable. Without sharing in the poise of Christ (cf. Jn. 10:18), 'the last state of our condition will always be worse than the first' (cf. Mt. 12:45). Only *in Christ* do we acquire the Presence of mind and heart to resist 'throwing the first stone' (cf. Jn. 8:7).

Objects in the world continually change and die. Acceptance of this fact brings immediate, surprising, peace. This peace is an affirmation that we are not identical with our bodies, and that we transcend both change and death. In Presence, our 'hope does not disappoint us because we feel God's love being poured into our hearts through the Holy Spirit' (cf. Rom. 5:5).

Without Presence, we are like wind chimes clanging in the breeze. Wind chimes may make beautiful sounds but they cannot make music. The music of heaven is heard only when we awaken to Presence. Presence is the space in which the 'songs of the angels' resound (cf. Isa. 6:3).

---

[66] See René Girard, *Things Hidden Since the Foundation of the World.*

In Presence, we acquire an arresting awareness that who we are is not identical with what we see or think or do. In Presence, God shows us that he has 'called us by name' and 'we belong to Christ as Christ belongs to God' (cf. Isa. 43:1; 1 Cor. 3:23).

In Presence, we are given to understand that creation *ex nihilo* does not mean that God made something out of a substance called 'nothing,' but that all that exists does so as an unconditioned effulgence imparted from a divine plenitude of God's uncreated Life. Even in our fallen state of existence, in Presence, we realize that God is 'all in all' (cf. Eph. 4:6; 1 Cor. 15:22-28).

Every time we make the present instant the focus of our undivided attention, we are transported into Presence. In Presence, it's as if the world stops and we step out of time and into the kingdom of God. 'Whether in the body or out of the body only God knows' (cf. 2 Cor.).

Presence is the voice of God beckoning us, 'If today you hear my voice, harden not your hearts' (cf. Ps. 95:7-8; Heb. 3:15; 4:7).

We can be happy anywhere because we can be present anywhere. One instant of Presence brings greater joy than a lifetime of achievement. 'One day within the courts' of Presence 'is worth a thousand elsewhere' (cf. Ps. 84:10).

Presence is the very definition of Love. In Presence, the other is received as other, creating a communion and intimacy established upon respect for alterity. Relationships founded on the bedrock of Presence 'cannot be shaken' (cf. Mt. 7:26).

We can't, it seems, have our cake and eat it too. That is, we cannot desire to *possess* an object and *love* it at the same time. In Presence, we relinquish our desire to possess; instead, we receive everything in love. (cf. 1 Cor. 4:7; 6:19). Covetousness kills, while Presence saves (cf. Ex. 20:17; Dt. 5:21).

Presence is the harrowing of hell. In Presence, the fires of hell are immediately extinguished by 'a fountain of living water' (cf. Jn. 7:38). The 'gates of hell cannot prevail' against the the power of Presence (cf. Mt. 16:18).

Presence is the *death of death* (cf. 1 Cor. 15:26). Once death is accepted as simply another event arising and dissolving in Presence, it ceases to threaten us. In Presence, every event is acceptable. In Presence, 'there is a time to live and a time to die, a time to keep and a time to cast away' (cf. Sir. 3:2, 6).

Experienced in Presence, death is a flower opening, a butterfly emerging. In Presence, no one 'takes our lives from us but we lay them down of our own accord, only to take them up again' (cf. Jn. 10:18).

Presence creates space for the other to be 'other'. This space is the breath of the Holy Spirit. In Presence, we become, in Christ, 'life-giving spirits' (cf. 1 Cor. 15:45).

In Presence, everything is allowed to be, just as it is. Presence is the power of allowance, of letting-be, of letting go. Presence, like God, is without judgment (cf. Jn. 5:22; 8:15). In the light of Presence, all things are judged rightly (cf. Rev. 16:7; 1 Cor. 2:15).

Letting-be-ness (*Gelassenheit*) is a synonym for Presence. *Gelassenheit* (or Presence) is a creative act of letting go issuing in an immediate effulgence of life and joy. There is no one who 'has let go of house or brothers or sisters or mother or father or children or lands who will not receive a hundredfold now in this time, and in the age to come eternal life' (cf. Mk. 10:29–30).

Presence is a mystery of *kenosis*: self-emptying, self-dispossession. In Presence, we divest ourselves of self-interest, while acquiring true self-possession. In Presence, we truly 'love our neighbor *as* we love ourselves' (cf. Mt. 19:19; Gal. 5:14).

Presence is not the absence of self-love but its perfection. Presence is a participation in God's own self-delight (cf. Mk. 1:11; 2 Pt. 1:17). In Presence, we love ourselves - and we love others - with the love with which it has pleased him to love us (cf. Prv. 8:31; Eph. 2:4; 1 Jn. 4:19).

Presence is the *sine quo non* of intimacy. Presence is the sophianic *ethos* in which alterity and communion become indivisibly unconfused. Presence is the connective tissue that makes possible our nuptial intimacy with Christ and forges our bonds of union with each other (cf. Eph. 5:25; Song 8:6).

Presence is an acid bath for our fears and anxieties. Presence is the 'lake of fire' (Rev. 19:20; 20:14-15; 21:8) burning away everything in us that is not of God. 'Nothing impure' is ever found in the mystery of Presence (cf. Rev. 21:27).

Suffering is our purgatorial preparation to enter the paradise of Presence. All suffering seems karmic and unending until we 'arise and return to the house of our father' (cf. Lk. 15:18). In Presence, we return to the Source and Satisfaction of our very existence.

From the infinite nothingness of God's self-dispossessing Life explodes everything that is. Because God is eternally dying to Godself, the universe is continually being born. The death of God within God (cf. Phil. 2:6-11) is Life for the life of the world (cf. Jn. 1:4; 6:51).

Presence has the power to dissolve the past. Memories - good or bad - are incinerated in the fires of the redemptive, present moment (cf. 1 Cor. 3:15). Presence makes 'all things new' (cf. Rev. 21:5)

All lesser loves - including those of family and friends (cf. Lk. 14:26; Mt. 19:27-28) - are rendered irrelevant in Presence. In Presence, whatever went before in our lives, or whatever may come after, appears as so much nothingness. In Presence, we 'forget what lies behind and strain forward to what lies ahead' (Php. 3:13).

Presence is an anagogical orientation to the *Plērōma* of our purpose for living. In Presence, we are already 'seated with Christ at the right hand of the Father' (cf. Eph. 1:20; 2:6; Col. 1:3). In Presence 'our minds are directed to things that are above, not to things that are on earth' (cf. Col. 3:1–2).

Christ is 'from above' and we are 'from below' (cf. Jn. 8:23). Presence traverses the 'unbridgeable chasm' separating us from God (cf. k. 16:26). In Presence, we 'who once were far off from him have been brought near to God' (cf. Eph. 2:13).

Our true identity is discovered in the sacred space of Presence. In Presence, we participate in a Power greater than ourselves which is *also* the form and essence of what we are. We are not God, yet we are one *with* God *in* the Mystery of Presence (cf. Jn. 17:21).

Our minds cannot know themselves, just as our eyes cannot see themselves. Both our minds and our eyes enjoy a Light which makes our knowing and seeing possible. That Light is Presence (cf. Ps. 36:9).

God is not identical with Presence, yet the experience of Presence affords our most immediate contact with God. Presence is the sophianic self-communication of God. Presence is the Wisdom of God, 'created in God from eternity, making its abode in the full assembly of the saints' (cf. Sir. 24:9–12).

Presence is filled with gentleness. In Presence, we experience the meaning of Jesus' words: 'I am meek and gentle of heart' (cf. Mt. 11:29).

Presence is a consciousness more prescient than conscience. Presence gives us discernment that transcends deliberation. Presence allows us to see all with the all-knowing, benevolent gaze of God (cf. Job 34:21; Nm. 24:16).

Abstraction and categorization have no place in the mystery of Presence. Everything beheld in Presence is absolutely singular. It is not only to Solomon, but to each of us, that God says, 'none like you has been before you and none like you shall arise after you (cf. 1 Kg. 3:12).

It is the mystery of being that touches us in Presence. Presence brings us a sense of our ontological origination in God. In Presence, we hear God's voice, as out of the whirlwind questioning Job: 'Who has given anything to me, that I should repay him? Does not everything under the whole heaven belong to me?' (cf. Job 41:11).

Presence unites and differentiates perfectly. In Christ, the many constitute the One, and One establishes the many (cf. Rom. 12:5; 1 Cor. 12:12). In Presence, 'we are to grow up in every way into him who is the head, into Christ (cf. Eph. 4:15).

Differentiation in Presence is the deified alternative to division, dialectic and dichotomy. Presence is an experience of 'otherness' without alienation, alterity without animosity. Presence is the space in which freedom and communion are reconciled as non-rivalrous twins (cf. Gen. 33:4). Presence is the place where 'mercy and faithfulness meet, where righteousness and peace kiss' (cf. Ps. 85:10).

Joy is the infallible sign of Presence. Divine bliss wells up spontaneously within us as, in Presence, we intuit the gratuity of being. In Presence, we echo Jesus' words, 'I thank thee, Father, Lord of heaven and earth, for hiding these things from the learned and wise, and revealing them to the simple' (cf. Lk 10:21; Ps. 138:1).

In Presence, we become increasingly transparent. In Presence, we are less preoccupied with self and more spontaneous with others. In Presence, there is nothing to hide (cf. Gen. 3:7-10). In Presence, we know 'that we are sufficient of ourselves to claim nothing as our own, but that all our sufficiency comes from God' (cf. 2 Cor. 3:5).

In Presence we would never dream of 'pursuing holiness'. In Presence, the whole enterprise of 'acquiring virtue' and 'becoming perfect' appears ludicrous. Instead, in Presence, we are humbly and gratefully aware that 'No one is good but God alone' (cf. Mk. 10:18), and that, of ourselves, we are but 'unprofitable servants' (cf. Lk. 17:10).

In Presence, it's not what we do but *how* we do it that matters. In Presence, how we do anything is how we do everything. Every thought, word and action done in Presence conveys a 'weight of glory' too impossibly beautiful to estimate (cf. 2 Cor. 7:14). When done in Presence, even in 'putting in our two cents' amounts to 'more than all others who are contributing' (cf. Mk. 12:43).

Presence gives us acute situational awareness, while affording us patience with an obtuse world. In Presence, we move from lamenting, with Jesus, 'How much longer must I be with this evil generation?' (cf. Mk. 9:19) to 'having compassion on the crowds, because they are harassed and helpless, like sheep without a shepherd' (cf. Mt. 9:36).

Presence is devoid of self-obsession but filled with self-awareness. Presence holds open the space for the other without fear or expectation. Presence is a mystery of wordless affirmation. In Presence, we are one with Jesus who 'bent down and wrote with his finger on the ground' until the animus of condemnation dissolved (cf. Jn. 8:6-9).

In Presence, we realize we do not belong to ourselves. In Presence, we experience a high degree of self-possession, but always as a gift (cf. Jn. 15:15; Rev. 2:27). In Presence, we see that 'I am' and 'you are' are indivisible in the great, primordial 'I AM' (cf. Ex. 3:14).

Presence waits for the perfect word, a word that comes, not from the self, but from a Source beyond the self. Nothing comes forth in Presence other than what is given. In Presence, 'even before a word is on my tongue, O Lord, you know it' (cf. Ps. 139:4).

It is impossible to script what comes from Presence. Any idea arising in Presence comes unbidden from the 'hidden depths' of God (cf. 1 Cor. 2:10). Presence 'imparts a secret and hidden wisdom of God, which God decreed before the ages for our glorification' (cf. 1 Cor. 2:7).

No one is more aware that all creative, artistic, inventive genius comes forth as a gift in Presence than the artist herself. Presence is a participation in the uncreated creativity of the One 'through whom all things were made, and without whom nothing that was made was made' (cf. Jn. 1:1–3).

In Presence, we grieve egoic, self-serving behavior in the same moment we forgive it. In Presence, we 'rise up with the queen of the south and with the prophet Jonah to condemn this generation' (cf. Lk. 11:31), while also saying with Christ, 'Father, forgive them, for they know not what they are doing' (cf. Lk. 23:34).

The briefest wafting of Presence breaks down the structure of our inner topography. The slightest breath of Presence overturns our habitual perspectives. Yet, Presence dismantles the crystallized patterns of our personal world only to reconstruct us as 'new creations' in Christ (cf. 2 Cor 5:17; Gal. 6:15). Presence is always given 'for building us up and never for destroying us' (cf. 2 Cor. 10:8).

Presence transforms pain into suffering. 'Suffer the children to come unto me' (cf. Lk. 18:16). Here we can see that a root meaning of 'suffering' is 'to allow'. Presence is the space of allowing that makes 'suffering' redemptive.

Presence is liberation from our 'slavery to the fear of death' (cf. Heb. 2:15). Presence mediates the deathless Spirit of the One who is 'the resurrection and the life' (cf. Jn. 11:25).

Presence inhabits the half-life of every instant. Presence reveals the Now as an indefinable point drawing us ever more deeply into the ineffable mystery of God. In Presence, we know that 'now is the acceptable time', now is the time 'to call upon God while he is still near' (cf. 2 Cor. 6:2; Isa. 55:6).

Presence expands outward even as it settles us more deeply into silence. Resting in Presence, we radiate peace beyond ourselves. In Presence, we communicate a peace 'the world cannot give' (cf. Jn. 14:27).

Presence functions like spiritual and social WD-40. Presence opens hearts that are bolted shut, lubricates relationships that are stuck. Friction is eliminated wherever Presence is applied. In Presence, 'the oil of salvation' cleanses those upon whom it is lavishly poured out (cf. Lv. 14:29; Sir. 9:8).

Presence is a space of epiphanic awareness. In Presence, wisdom, insights and revelations arrive unbidden in the intentional emptiness of Presence. In Presence, 'that which has not been told us we shall see, and that which we have not heard we shall understand' (cf. Isa. 52:15).

Presence precludes transactional living. There is no 'if-then' in Presence. In Presence, God's Word is never 'Yes and No; but always Yes' (cf. 2 Cor. 1:19).

Presence is allergic to exhortation and invective. Nothing is more alien to Presence than moralism. Presence is such a participation in the ecstasy of God such that 'the wisdom of this world' - even its ethical wisdom - appears as 'pure folly with God' (cf. 1 Cor. 3:19).

Presence is inherently promissory. Devoid of pressure, Presence promises only good.

Presence is pregnant with an eschatological plenitude of light, love and joy. In Presence, we 'seize the hope set before us, securing a sure and steadfast anchor for our souls' (cf. Heb. 6:18–20).

Presence is inherently redemptive, fastening on every failure as an opportunity for salvific self-transcendence. In Presence, we see that even death is desired by God 'so that the Son of God may be glorified by means of it as the resurrection and the life' (cf. Jn. 11:4, 25).

Presence reveals evil, not as the equal and opposite of goodness, but as its absence. Evil is always a 'privation,' never something substantial. Evil has no power of its own, save that of deception. In Presence, we can say to those apoplectic about the 'existence' of evil in the world: 'You are very much mistaken' (cf. Mk. 12:27).

Presence imparts a certain pedagogical patience. In Presence, even our missteps seem those of an infant learning to walk. In Presence, we 'forgive as we have been forgiven' (cf. Col. 3:13). In Presence, we 'encourage the fainthearted, help the weak, and are patient with them all' (cf. 1 Th. 5:14).

Presence engenders a genuine and abiding sense of humor. If, as Chesterton says, 'angels can fly because they take themselves lightly,'[67] they do so abiding in the Presence of God (cf. Lk. 1:19). In Presence, life is taken seriously, but 'with a grain of salt' added for flavor (cf. Lk. 14:24).

Presence reveals despair, dejection and depression as negligible, unnecessary and ignorant. In Presence, we spend no time bemoaning our stupidity; instead, we subvert it with acceptance and good humor. In Presence, 'those who once sowed in tears now reap with joy!' (cf. Ps. 126:5).

---

[67] G. K. Chesterton, *Orthodoxy*.

Presence is such that 'the gates of Hades will not prevail against it' (cf. Mt. 16:18). Barriers of self-interest and fear-driven defensiveness cannot prevent the power of Presence from blowing away the bastions of our sinful selves (cf. Mt. 7:27). In Presence, our lives are 'built on rock' which no wind nor waves can destroy (cf. Lk. 6:48).

Presence is the key that both unlocks the 'gates of Hades' (cf. Mt. 16:18) to 'set the captives free' (cf. Lk. 4:18), and opens the doors to the kingdom of God (cf. Mt. 16:19). Presence is the guarantee that the gates of heaven will 'never be shut' (cf. Rev. 21:25).

In Presence, we never find fault or indulge in accusation. At the same time, Presence makes us acutely aware of evil as the absence of Presence. In Presence, we agonize with Christ over the sins of the world, and share in his resolve to 'love our enemies and bless those who persecute us' (cf. Mt. 5:44).

Presence has no equal or opposite. Presence is the Light beyond our notions of good and evil, revealing both as imposters. 'No one is good but God alone' (cf. Lk. 18:19) and God's love 'shines on the evil and the good alike' (cf. Mt. 5:45).

Presence reveals evil as the absence of Presence. . Presence reveals evil as a privation, lacking in positive substance.[68] Presence reveals evil as an empty deception that includes accusation, lies and murder (cf. Jn. 8:44). Presence is the light of God that dispels and 'conquers the darkness' (cf. Jn. 1:5).

---

[68] As St. Augustine said: For what is that which we call evil but the absence of good? ... For evil has no positive nature; but the loss of good has received the name 'evil' (*Enchiridion; City of God, Book XI*).

Presence reveals the demonic as our inclination to demonize. In Presence, we refuse to accuse, to indict, to scapegoat. In Presence, we resist the temptation to 'exchange an eye for an eye' (cf. Dt. 19:21; Mt. 5:38) or to judge those who have misjudged us (cf. Lk. 6:37). In Presence, we overcome evil, not by fighting fire with fire (cf. Mk. 3:23; Rom. 12:21), but with the 'living water' that flows from the pierced heart of Jesus (cf. Jn. 19:34).

Presence awakens us to the performative power of language.[69] In Presence, we realize our utterances are actions, not just words. In Presence, we no longer waste our breath with anodyne speech. In Presence, we 'bless, we never curse' (cf. Rom. 12:14). In Presence, we 'pray for our persecutors' rather than provoke them (cf. Lk. 6:28).

Presence is the power of God that compels 'Hades to give up its dead' (cf. Rev. 20:13). In Presence, those who 'dwell in the dust of their sins awaken and sing for joy!' (cf. Isa. 26:19). Presence 'gives light to those who sit in darkness and the shadow of death, guiding their feet into the way of peace' (cf. Lk. 1:79).

Presence is the remedial, redemptive, restorative, relentlessly consuming fire of God. (cf. Dt. 4:24; Heb. 12:29). In Presence, all that is not of God is burned away so we ourselves can be saved from the prolonged suffering from our sins (cf. 1 Cor. 3:15; 2 Pt. 3:10).

---

[69] See John Austin, *How to Do Things with Words,* and John Searle, *Speech Acts.*

We witness to Presence always, using words only when necessary. In Presence, we show rather than tell. In Presence, it is natural for us to show that actions speak louder than words (cf. Mt. 23:3).

Presence is like water, always seeking the deepest, darkest, lowest place with its life-giving power. Nothing penetrates more deeply than Presence. In Presence, Christ descends into the depths of our being 'to set the captives free' (cf. Lk. 4:18; Ps. 146:7).

Presence buoys up and saves all that has fallen down. In the absolute blackness of failure, Presence appears as a promissory light. In Presence, 'those who walk in darkness see a great light, and upon those who dwell in a land of deep darkness, a light shines' (cf. Isa. 9:2).

Presence unleashes imagination. In Presence, solutions to our problems spontaneously suggest themselves, often with disarming simplicity. In Presence, it is the wisdom of God that teaches us (cf. Wis. 7:22), making us 'keen in judgment' (cf. Wis. 8:11).

In Presence, nothing is a dead end. Instead, dead ends become occasions of grace. In Presence, powerlessness is a catalyst to surrender to a power greater than ourselves. In Presence, we are 'content with weaknesses, insults, hardships, persecutions, and calamities; for when we are weak, we are strong' (cf. 2 Cor. 12:10).

Preachers and teachers would do well to spend more time in Presence than analyzing texts. Without Presence, we 'teach as doctrines the precepts of men and discuss God in vain' (cf. Mk. 7:7). In Presence, by contrast, we experience 'truth in our inward being and receive wisdom in the recesses of our heart' (cf. Ps. 51:6).

Presence often provokes as much outrage as it inspires admiration. The collision of Presence with unconsciousness is not always a pretty picture. Presence is a 'stumbling block' for many (cf. 1 Cor. 1:23), often alienating members of our own families (cf. Mt. 10:36). 'Blessed are those who find no *skandalon*'[70] in Presence (cf. Lk. 7:23).

Presence is a 'two-edged sword' (cf. Heb. 4:12), causing division even as it seeks to generate concord (cf. Lk. 12:51). Established in Presence, we can 'come to our own' and find they 'receive us not' (cf. Jn. 1:11). But with 'everyone who does receive us, we become deified children of God' (cf. Jn. 1:12).

Presence prompts some to double-down on their obstreperousness, while others awaken to a new day. No promoter of Presence is welcome in the hometown of the ego (cf. Lk. 4:24).

---

[70] *Skandalon* is the Greek term translated as 'stumbling block'. To be 'scandalized' means to be attracted to something or someone one both admires and detests. *Skandalon* exercises a hypnotically frustrating effect on those who suffer from it. For more analysis of this important topic, see: *René Girard and the New Testament Use of Skandalon* at: http://girardianlectionary.net/learn/girard-on-skandalon.

In Presence, consciousness and conscience elide. In Presence, doing the right next thing becomes second-nature. In Presence, we 'have no need that any one should teach us' since, in Presence, we are 'all taught by God' (cf. 1 Jn. 2:27; Jn. 6:45).

With moralists, conscience sometimes acquires a bad name, retaining overtones of a harsh and demanding heteronomy. In ethics, the 'you should's' often overshadow the 'you can's'. It is not that way in Presence. In Presence, 'our goodness is not by compulsion but of our own free will' (cf. Phlmn. 14).

In Presence, it's as impossible to reject what is good as it is for a man dying of thirst in the desert to refuse to drink from an oasis. Abiding in Presence, it is virtually impossible for us to do what is contrary to truth. In Presence, we 'see clearly' (cf. Mk. 8:25; Mt. 7:5). In Presence, we 'know the truth that sets us free' (cf. Jn. 8:32) from quandary and indecision.

Presence is a transformative Source of love that bewilders those who think primarily in terms of right and wrong. Presence is at once the indictment and exoneration of all ethical systems. Presence does not 'abolish the law but perfects it' (cf. Mt. 5:17; Rom. 3:31).

Presence is a mystery that takes us beyond good and evil. Presence is an experience of deifying beauty that issues in edifying behavior almost as an afterthought. Established in Presence, we accrue virtue as a by-product. Abiding in Presence, 'the seeds sprout and grow, we know not how' (cf. Mk. 4:27).

Presence is a swirling river of inspiring cross-currents. In Presence, we are moved this way and that, never stagnating in thought, always carried forward in hope. Presence is the 'river of life' that carries us, willy-nilly, into the heart of the 'heavenly Jerusalem' (cf. Rev. 21:2).

In Presence, 'a great light from heaven suddenly shines about us', blinding us to the world and opening us to God (cf. Acts 9:4). Like St. Paul, we remain in the dark until, in Presence, 'the cataracts fall' from our spiritual vision (cf. Acts 9:18).

In Presence, we acquire a 'mature wisdom that is not a wisdom of this age or of the rulers of this age, who are doomed to pass away' (cf. 1 Cor. 2:6).

Once we have come to trust the power of Presence to transform any situation from darkness into light, we return to Presence as often as possible. We have found 'the one thing needful' and, by God's grace, will 'not have it taken from us' (cf. Lk. 10:42).

Familiarity with Presence is such that even our falls from Presence precipitate our immediate return. 'Where can we go from God's Spirit, or where can we flee from his presence?' (Ps. 139:7). In Presence, God 'raises up what is fallen and rebuilds what is in ruins' (cf. Am. 9:11). Life in Presence is a constant experience of redemptive awareness.

Presence is the path to joy, and joy is the fruit of Presence (cf. Jn. 17:13; Php. 2:2).

Presence bathes us in a supernal light of infinite blessing. In Presence, a deified perspective arises that affords promise and hope in the direst of circumstances. In Presence, 'the God of hope that never disappoints fills us with all joy and peace' (cf. Rom. 5:5; 15:13).

Presence is 'a jealous lover' (cf. Ex. 34:14). Presence commands our undivided attention and issues in our unconditional surrender. In Presence, we identify with Jeremiah: 'You have seduced me, O God, and I have let myself be seduced' (cf. Jer. 20:7).

When we give ourselves to Presence, it gives everything to us. When, in Presence, we say to God, 'I am yours, and all that I have' (cf. 1 Kg. 20:4), God says to us, 'you are always with me, and all that is mine is yours' (cf. Lk. 15:31).

Presence is a sacrament of holy communion in which otherness and union meet, freedom and love kiss (cf. Ps. 85:10). Presence is the divine *Sophia* in which the world is in God and God in the world, without the world being God, nor God the world. In Presence we apprehend the unity of all things in God (cf. Acts 17:28; Eph. 1:23; 4:6).

Presence is the sacred space of eternal allowing in which alterity flourishes and alienation is unknown. Presence is an arena of acceptance where distinctions stand out but divorce does not occur. Presence is the 'new creation' (cf. Isa. 65:17) where 'lion and lamb' learn to live together in love (cf. Isa. 11:6-7).

Nothing can be forced in Presence. Presence involves an attentiveness that is at once effortful and effortless. In Presence, we remain open yet empty, alert but relaxed. Presence is a space of virginal vigilance (cf. Mt. 25:1ff.), confident in the One who 'remembers his promises of mercy forever' (cf. Lk. 1:55).

Even if the concept of 'God' can no longer do so, Presence remains undiminished in its power to communicate a why-less love. Presence is what Presence does. Is Presence 'not allowed to do what it chooses with what belongs to it? Or, do we begrudge the groundless generosity' we experience abiding in Presence? (cf. Mt. 20:15).

In Presence, there are no head-on collisions. No one comes into Presence 'to test or to argue' (cf. 1 Kg. 10:1; Mk. 10:2). In Presence, whatever has gone awry is made right again in an ocean of mercy (cf. Lk. 5:4-11), not in a whirlwind of might (cf. 1 Kg. 19:11).

In Presence, we remain unperturbed but not indifferent. Presence sharpens our moral and aesthetic senses, while sublating them within a higher, accepting and forgiving love. In Presence, we are given the grace to 'bless those who revile and persecute us, to rejoice and be glad', knowing prophets of Presence are 'always so persecuted' (cf. Mt. 5:11–12).

Presence is a bottomless depth of understanding and compassion. In Presence, the 'us vs. them' dichotomy is overcome. In Presence, we empathize without absorption, care without becoming co-dependent. In Presence, we 'belong neither to Paul nor Apollo but to Christ' in whom all things co-inhere without competition (cf. 1 Cor. 1:12).

Presence is the 'fiery furnace' in which the whole of humanity (i.e., 'the Son of Man') is incandescently in communion with the tri-personal God (cf. Dan. 3:23ff.). In Presence, we are painfully purified with the 'consuming fire' of God's love, restored to the eschatological beauty envisioned for us by God 'before the foundation of the world' (cf. Eph. 1:4).

Theosis is the outcome of abiding in Presence, and Presence the *ethos* of *theosis*. Presence is the greenhouse of 'God's garden', beautifying in every season those whose fruit-bearing leaves provide 'healing for the nations' (cf. 1 Cor. 3:9; Rev. 22:2).

Presence reveals compassion not primarily as an ethical good but as an ontological given. There is something primordially awe-full about Presence, of which 'being good' is a poor facsimile. In Presence, all notions of goodness are relativized by the transfiguring Light of Christ (cf. Lk. 18:19; Isa. 55:8).

Presence manifests a Source of benevolence beyond our genealogy of morals. In Presence, dichotomies of good vs evil, clean vs unclean, friend vs foe are overcome (cf. Mt. 5:45). Presence is the 'silence of Christ' in which the saint and sinner join hands in humble adoration before him (cf. Rev. 8:1; Lk. 22:59).

Grim determination finds no purchase in Presence. Presence is a flow, not an effort or a grind. The delicate kiss of Presence softens the stiffest upper lip; the gentle touch of Presence dissolves the strongest iron grip. In Presence, the 'highest mountains and the everlasting hills' of our pride are 'made low', and the valleys' of self-hatred are 'filled up so that we may walk safely in the glory of God' (cf. Bar. 5:7).

Everything touched by Presence is instantly redeemed. The kindly light of Presence softens the hardest stare, melts the stoniest heart. No created power can resist the liquifying power of Presence. In the end, Presence will be 'all in all' (cf. 1 Cor. 15:28).

Presence is a purgatory of grief and a paradise of gratitude. In Presence, we grieve the violence of the world yet rejoice at being immersed in an ocean of love. In Presence, we experience the 'time of our visitation' that the world has missed (cf. Wis. 3:7l; Lk. 19:44).

Presence inclines us more and more to silence. In Presence, we are loathe to utter clichés or unconsciously opine. Presence reminds us of our mothers' motto: 'If you have nothing good to say, say nothing at all'. In Presence, we find it impossible to 'return evil for evil'. Instead, 'we bless and do not curse' what is wrong with the world (cf. 1 Pt. 3:9).

Abiding in Presence, we exude Presence. In Presence, we serve as God's air-freshener. In Presence, we are, as it were, 'the first fruits' (cf. 1 Cor, 15:20-23) of God's 'abundant harvest' (cf. Mt. 9:37), 'offered on the altar' of the world 'for a pleasing fragrance' (cf. Lev. 2:12).

Presence is the existential locus of our external, religious rites. Presence is the emptiness of the 'Holy of Holies' (cf. Heb. 9:3), and the Cloud reposing upon the 'Mercy Seat' (cf. Ex. 37:9). Presence is an appearance of the risen Christ who 'comes suddenly into the temple' of our hearts (cf. Mal. 3:1).

Presence is the fullness of God's future (*Plērōma*) unveiling itself in real time. In Presence, the infinite horizon of God's promises to Abraham (cf. Gen. 12) are proleptically disclosed in the half-life of every present moment. In Presence, we catch a glimpse of 'the plans God has for us; plans for our welfare and not for evil', the promise of 'a future and a hope' (cf. Jer. 29:11).

In Presence, we experience a simultaneous self-emptying and self-fulfillment. In Presence, we like the 'streams that run to the sea, but the sea is never full'. In Presence, we 'return to the place from which the stream within us runs, only to run again' (cf. Sir. 1:7).

Abiding in Presence means cherishing the blessed unfoldment of every present moment. Abiding in Presence, we are set free from 'worrying about what we are to eat or what we are to wear' (cf. Mt. 6:31). We acquire the trust of 'the lilies of the field and the birds of the air' (cf. Mt. 6:26-29). We are given 'whatever is needed day by day without fail' (cf. Ezra 6:9).

Presence is an interior darkness in which the light of Christ appears. Presence is the 'gentle silence enveloping all things' from which God's 'all-powerful Word leaps from heaven', taking his 'royal throne' within our souls, redeeming lives that are otherwise 'doomed' (cf. Wis. 18:14–15).

Presence is the alchemical crucible in which our leaden hearts are turned to gold (cf. Prv. 17:3; Ezek. 11:9). Presence is the purifying fire of God's divine mercy in which our hearts of coal are turned into immortal diamonds.[71] In Presence, we become 'a crown of beauty in the hand of the Lord, and a royal diadem in the hand of our God' (cf. Isa. 62:3).

Presence backlights the lives of those who abide in it. A saint's halo is a nimbus of a life lived in Presence. In Presence, we are transformed 'from one degree of glory to another' (cf. 2. Cor. 3:18). In Presence, we become 'the praise of his glory' (cf. Eph. 1:12-14).

Presence is the indefinable locus of our deification. In Presence, we hear God telling us, 'You are gods' (cf. Ps. 82:6; Jn. 10:34).

Presence is a simultaneous seeking and satisfaction. Presence feeds our insatiable hunger for the Infinite with the 'bread that comes down from heaven' (cf. Jn. 6:50). In Presence, we seek after God with the same passion that Mary and Joseph 'sought after Jesus among their kinsfolk and acquaintances' (cf. Lk. 2:44). Presence is the unending fulfillment of the promise, 'seek and you will find' (cf. Lk. 11:9).

In Presence, our souls become 'the Eden of God' (cf. Gen. 2:8; 1 Cor. 3:9) in which 'the Lord God walks among the trees of the garden in the cool of the day' (cf. Gen. 3:8).

---

[71] See Richards Rohr, *Immortal Diamond, The Search for our True Self.* See also: https://sciencestruck.com/how-does-coal-become-diamond

In Presence, we are 'enflamed but not immolated' by the consuming fire of God's love (cf. Ex. 3:2). In Presence, we become living theophanies of God's glory. In Presence, those we encounter 'are on holy ground' (cf. Ex. 3:5).

Presence is an invisible mesh that makes humanity a seamless whole within itself and with God. The 'Son of Man' includes, in his very personhood as the God-man, the whole of the human race. 'One like a Son of Man" in the fiery furnace is the *Totus Christus* in deified communion with the tri-personal God (cf. Dan. 3:23).

Presence is the indefinable power that makes possible our conscious connection with nature. 'I said to the almond tree, 'Sister, speak to me of God'. And the almond tree blossomed'.[72]

Presence is the space in which we allow reality to 'present itself' on its own terms. Presence reveals 'otherness' as the condition for, not an adumbration of, a prior unity. In Presence, the infinite variety and utter singularity of creation is experienced as a sacrament of God's differentiated personhood in triune unity (cf. Dan. 15:34-63).

Presence is the space where alterity is permitted and otherness shines forth in irreducible and irreplaceable beauty. Presence is the space where alienation and opposition are unknown. In Presence, 'the lion reclines with the lamb and the leopard with the calf' (cf. Isa. 11:6; 65:25).

---

[72] Nikos Kazantzakis, *Report to Greco.*

Presence disabuses us of our *need* to help others. There is no compulsivity in Presence, including running to someone's rescue. In Presence, we exhibit the kind of love that enabled Jesus, even when Lazarus whom Jesus 'loved was critically ill', 'to remain where he was for two more days' (cf. Jn. 11:6).

Compassion is communicated only through Presence. In Presence, we recognize the power of healing comes not *from* us but *through* us. In Presence, we hear Jesus say, 'do not rejoice that the spirits are subject to you; rejoice rather that your names are written in heaven' (cf. Lk. 10:19–20).

Presence is a space of innocent perception. In Presence, our vision is continually refreshed. In Presence, we acquire a kind of second naïveté, i.e., we see with the eyes of a child now imbued with the wisdom of a sage (cf. Mt. 10:16).

All is intuitively known in Presence. In Presence, awe and wonder replace worry and anxiety. The fundamental ok-ness of life pervades the space of Presence. In Presence, our only thought is 'Lord, it is good for us to be here' (cf. Mk. 9:5).

Thoughts assault Presence like soldiers an enemy fortress. Such thoughts are easily dispatched if the moat of our awareness is expansive enough. Presence is the 'great chasm' preventing thoughts from disturbing our heavenly bliss (cf. Mt. 10:16).

Presence gives us an acute anticipation of an unanticipated fullness of love (*Plērōma*). In Presence, we intuit an implicit cosmic consummation that brings us continuous joy. Presence is the space in which hope springs eternal (cf. Rom. 5:5; Prv. 23:18; Sir. 14:2).

Presence is an interior 'land of milk and honey' (cf. Ex. 3:8). Presence is the honey that sweetens every sadness, the milk that mystically strengthens weary bones (cf. Jer. 20:9). Presence is 'sweetness to the soul and health to the body' (cf. Prv. 16:24). In Presence, we 'taste and see the goodness of the Lord' (cf. Ps. 34:8).

In Presence, we are both aware of our moods and transcend them. Presence allows us to experience emotional fluctuations while at the same time sublating them in an ocean of God's benign acceptance. In Presence, Christ 'takes us by the hand, lifts us up and our fever leaves us' (cf. Mk. 1:31).

In Presence, our emotional inconstancy is acknowledged and overcome. In Presence, we experience the strength that comes from seeing our weaknesses and simply accepting them. Presence is the sophianic power that allows us to say, 'I am content with my weaknesses, for when I am weak, then I am strong' (cf. 2 Cor. 12:10).

We experience the power of Presence to the degree to which we give ourselves over to it. The smallest seed of Presence 'bears fruit in abundance' (cf. Jn. 15:5). If, however, Presence 'finds no place in us' (cf. Jn. 8:37), Christ 'can do no mighty work there' (cf. Mk. 6:5).

Presence is the tacit Source of illumination of everything we see, yet Presence forever escapes our conceptual grasp. When we attempt to hold onto Presence, it 'passes through our midst and goes away' (cf. Lk. 4:30). Presence is the appearance of the risen Christ, saying, 'Do not cling to me' (cf. Jn. 20:17).

In Presence, we experience a certain ecstasy about the very 'is-ing-ness' of things. In Presence, we delight in the unconditioned beauty of every moment. Every minute we abide in Presence seems like 'the beginning of God's creation' (Rev. 3:14).

In Presence, everything seems perfect by virtue of the sheer fact of its here-and-now-ness. Presence is an 'intuition of being' that brings infinite bliss. In Presence, we cannot but believe that nothing 'in all creation will be able to separate us from the love of God in Christ Jesus our Lord (cf. Rom. 8:39).

In Presence, we *belong* to that which we *behold*. Presence is an experience of communion with all that is other from us. In Presence, we receive others 'no longer as slaves' to our projections, but 'as beloved brothers and sisters in the Lord' (cf. Phlmn. 16).

Presence calls us to ever-greater simplicity. In Presence, inner poverty is spiritual fecundity. Abiding in Presence, we know we 'have nothing that we did not receive, and that, if we have received it as a gift, there is no room for boasting' (cf. 1 Cor. 4:7). At the same time, we rejoice that 'having nothing of our own, we possess everything' (cf. 2 Cor. 6:10).

Presence beckons us to an ever-deeper silence that is also an increase in awareness. In Presence, we are inwardly poised to hear 'the voice of the beloved!' (cf. Song 2:8).

In Presence, we are reduced to a still-point of infinite openness. In Presence, our attentiveness is as intense as our expectations are absent. In Presence, we 'give our ears to the inner Wisdom of the Lord and incline our ears to the words of his mouth' (cf. Ps. 78:1).

We enter Presence like storybook characters entering a secret passage. Susan and Edmund discover nothing in Narnia[73] as enchanting and transforming as what we happen upon in Presence. In Presence, we discover 'the mystery hidden for ages' (cf. Col. 1:26), 'the secret things that belong to the Lord our God' (cf. Dt. 29:29).

Devoid of expectations, Presence is also the end of resentment. In Presence we recognize expectations as nothing but premeditated resentments. In Presence, we never 'grumble that the last will be first, and the first last' (cf. Mt. 20:11, 16). Instead, we delight that God 'desires all be saved and come to a knowledge of his truth' (cf. 2 Tim. 21:4).

Resistance to reality - and its attendant anxiety - dissolves in Presence. In Presence, we embrace the fact we 'cannot add one cubit to our span of life' (cf. Mt. 6:27). In Presence, we know 'the Lord has made everything for its purpose, even the wicked for the day of trouble' (cf. Prv. 16:4). In Presence, we account it a blessing 'the day's own trouble is sufficient for the day' (cf. Mt. 6:34).

---

[73] C. S. Lewis, *The Lion, the Witch and the Wardrobe.*

Presence is 'death to sin but life in the Spirit' (cf. Rom. 8:6). Presence is the death of self-interest but the birth of humble self-possession. In Presence, we become as nothing, yet feel more fulfilled than ever. In Presence, we know ourselves as 'unprofitable servants' (cf. Lk. 17:10) to whom 'it has pleased God to give the whole of his kingdom' (cf. Lk. 12:32).

Relaxing into Presence is an endless, nuptial adventure. In Presence, we know 'I am my beloved's and my beloved is mine' (cf. Song 2:16; 6:3).

Presence is an experience of ever-deeper relinquishment, of ever-greater surrender. In Presence, surrender is victory, self-forgetfulness is self-discovery. In Presence, we discover that when we let go we are 'lifted up and seated with Christ in the heavenly places' (cf. Eph. 2:6).

In Presence, the other's joy is our joy, the other's sorrow our sorrow. In Presence, we know ourselves as more than 'our brother's keeper' (cf. Gen. 4:9). In Presence, we 'love our neighbor as ourselves' (cf. Mt. 22:39) both literally and figuratively. In Presence, we experience ourselves as 'members one of another' in the *Totus Christus* (cf. Eph. 4:25).

Presence prevents us from falling into possessiveness. In Presence, the sinful powers of covetousness - 'the lust of the eyes' (1 Jn. 2:16) - are held at bay.

Presence is an *ethos* of empathy without the pathos. Presence is perfect compassion without condescension. Presence is the perfect synergy of 'be perfect as your father in heaven is perfect' (cf. Mt. 5:48) and 'forgive your brother seventy times seven' (cf. Mt. 18:22).

Presence communicates supreme confidence, both in ourselves and in the One who possesses us in Presence. In Presence, we know we 'can do all things in Christ who strengthens us' (cf. Php. 4:13). At the same time, we know that 'apart from him we can do nothing' (cf. Jn. 15:5).

In Presence, we are like a mother listening to her infant's baby monitor, but without worry. Presence is an expectant openness, devoid of fear and suffused with love. In Presence, we are perfectly attuned to 'the voice of of the beloved' (cf. Song 2:8).

Presence is an interior listening that suspends thought. It is impossible to be fully present and analyze at the same time. In Presence, we assume the posture of Samuel: 'Speak, Lord, your servant is listening' (cf. 1 Sam. 3:10).

Presence is the place of selfless self-possession. We are never more in control of ourselves than in Presence, yet never less occupied with ourselves. In Presence, we 'lay down our lives only to take them up again' (cf. Jn. 10:17).

In Presence, our self-awareness and self-appreciation expand, while our self-interest and self-obsession recede. In Presence, we share in the joy and generosity of Zacchaeus (cf. Lk. 19:1-10). In Presence, we hear the voice of Christ: 'Today salvation has come to this house' (cf. Lk. 19:9).

Presence is a place of intentional unknowing. Presence is a space of deliberate forgetfulness. In Presence, we experience God 'putting his laws in our hearts, and remembering our sins and misdeeds no longer' (cf. Heb. 10:16–17).

Presence is the place of no agenda, no expectations, no preconceptions. Presence is the place of surprise where nothing, and everything, is always new (cf. Rev. 21:5). Presence is the *ethos* of 'the new creation' (cf. Isa. 65:17).

Presence is a participation in the wise prudence of Gamaliel (cf. Acts 5:34-39). Presence imbues us with the sentiment of the sage: 'A gentle answer turns away wrath' (Prv. 15:1).

Presence is a soft afternoon light burnishing our lives with a supernal beauty. Presence is the benign smile of a grandfather watching his grandchildren play. Presence is the dying of the wind, allowing the sound to carry across the waters of our souls.

Presence is filled with unnameable promise. Presence gives us unbounded hope. In Presence, we intuit the 'dearest deep-down freshness of things'.[74] In Presence, we receive a proleptic sense of a final, glorious *Plērōma* in which God will be 'all in all' (cf. 1 Cor. 15:28).

Presence is an electrically-charged eschatological awareness. Presence is a sense that the 'fullness of time' (cf. Gal. 4:4; Eph. 1:10) has already arrived and is yet still to come. Presence is a pregnant expectation of a cosmic *Apokatastasis* which 'no eye has seen, nor ear heard, nor human mind ever imagined' (cf. 1 Cor. 2:9; Isa. 64:4).

Presence is the space of true 'for-giveness'. In Presence, we 'give the benefit of the doubt' to another even before it is requested. Presence is, as it were, love paid forward in the form of unrestricted, non-judgmental openness (cf. 1 Jn. 4:10; Rom. 5:8).

Presence is the space of alert repose. Presence is the indefinable nexus where *kairos* redeems *chronos*. Presence is the place where 'timing is everything' yet 'time means nothing'. Presence is the place where 'we find forgiveness' (cf. Sir. 18:20) and 'shine forth like sparks running through stubble' (cf. Wis. 3:7).

---

[74] A phrase from Gerard Manley Hopkins' poem, *God's Grandeur*.

To discover Presence is the spiritual equivalent of the mathematical discovery of zero. Nothing in itself, Presence infuses meaning into all moments that count as time. Presence is the unthematic horizon of infinite light and love in which 'we live and move and have our being' (cf. Acts 17:28).

Presence is as undefinable and indivisible as the apex of an arching arrow or a ball tossed in the air. Presence is akin to the point of zero gravity at the epicenter of a teeter-totter. Presence is the virginal point at the deepest center of who we are - the *Le Point Vierge* - where our humanity and the Mystery of divinity intersect.

Presence is an instrument used by the divine weaver who 'severs the last thread' (cf. Isa. 38:12) of our attachment to the 'works of the flesh' (Gal. 5:19; cf. Sir. 39:19). In Presence, we share in 'the mind that was in Christ Jesus' (cf. Php. 2:9).

Presence penetrates, permeates, and renders transparent those who give themselves over to it. In Presence, we are spiritually 'naked without shame' (cf. Gen. 2:5). In Presence, all shame and guilt is removed and we are covered over with garments, not 'of skins' (cf. Gen. 3:21), but of the Spirit (cf. Eph. 6:11; Rev. 3:18).

We remain spiritually blind if we do not see and feel the delicate but absolute difference between thinking and Presence. What Presence unveils is forever hidden from cognition (cf. Mt. 11:25). Apart from Presence, we wander aimlessly in the desert of our own self-deception.

Our transfiguration in Presence makes building 'tabernacles' to capture the experience of God's *Shekinah* (cf. Mk. 9:5) an exercise in well-intentioned idiocy. Abiding in Presence, we realize the time has come to 'worship God no longer in Jerusalem' or on any specific mountaintop but only 'in Spirit and in truth' (cf. Jn. 4:23-24).

Some believe the real Presence of God can be contained in tabernacles of gold. But like the *Shekinah* of God leading the Israelites in the desert (cf. Ex. 13:22) and the Holy Spirit 'blowing where it will' (cf. Jn. 3:8), God's Presence cannot be so constrained. As a manifestation of the risen Christ, Presence alights upon us 'at an hour we do not expect' and in persons and places we cannot imagine (cf. Lk. 12:40; Heb. 13:2).

Presence suffuses us as light a crystal clear window, or fire an incandescent log. Presence is the means of our 'divinization'.[75] In Presence, we realize the humble yet glorious truth that 'we are gods' in God (cf. 82:6; Jn. 10:34).

The transfiguring effect of Presence is altogether unrelated to the moral or ethical conduct. Presence is the immediate dissolution of our sins. Presence is the purest form of real for-giveness. In Presence, we apprehend that we have been healed and absolved from our sins even before we ask (cf. Mt. 9:1-8).

---

[75] See St. John of the Cross, *The Ascent of Mount Carmel*, II, 5, 6; *The Living Flame of Love*, I, 4, 19-24. Also, St. Athanasius, *On the Incarnation*, 54.

In Presence, we instantly rise above whatever depths of deprivation our personal lives may have fallen into. In Presence, we see that 'the world judges by appearances but God knows our hearts' (cf. Prv. 21:2; 1 Jn. 3:20). In Presence, we know that what is admired among men and women is often 'an abomination in the sight of God' (cf. Lk. 16:15). Conversely, what is considered as 'foolishness' by the world can be very 'precious in the eyes of God' (cf. 1 Cor. 1:18; 3:19).

Presence is the space in which we stand back from ourselves in a *diastasis* of salvific bliss. In Presence, peace arises. Presence is the 'dark, silent night' of our souls where 'all is calm, all is bright'.[76]

Would that a critical mass of humanity awaken to the mystery of Presence! What a miracle it would be if our weary world would 'lift up its eyes' to Presence and see that our 'salvation is close to hand' (cf. Lk 21:28; 2 Cor. 6:2). Such would be an apocalyptic event worth waiting for (cf. Mt. 24:36).

In Presence, questions about God's wisdom do not arise. No one in Presence ever asks: 'Why does God allow so much suffering?' or 'Why doesn't God do something about the world situation?'. Presence reveals such inquiries as unimportant and ultimately impertinent. So long as we insist in questioning God, he 'answers us not a word' (cf. Job 40:2; Isa. 36:21; Mt. 15:23; 27:14).

Presence is the bubble wrap in which our fragile world is cushioned. Wrapped in Presence, we have less chance of breaking the bruised reed or quenching the smoldering wick (cf. Isa. 42:3; Mt. 12:20).

---

[76] Cf. John of the Cross, *Dark Night of the Soul.*

Presence is the place where God relieves us of our fears, doubts and insecurities. In Presence, our shame and guilt about the past and anxiety and worries about the future find no foothold. In Presence, our questions, expectations, and pre-judgments are banished. In Presence, we hear God say, 'Go in peace, your trust has made you well' (cf. Lk. 8:48).

Presence is the hand of God, gently reaching into our world (cf. Lk. 11:20), to 'uphold all who are falling, and raising up all who are bowed down' (Ps. 145:14). Presence is the gentle rain of God, 'falling on the just and unjust alike' (cf. Mt. 5:45), refreshing those 'dying of thirst' (cf. Isa. 5:3; Jn. 6:35). To those who know its salvific power, Presence is 'as welcome as clouds of rain in the time of drought' (cf. Sir. 35:20).

In Presence, we become 'poor in spirit' but spiritually enriched (cf. Mt. 5:3). In Presence, we are emptied of our attachments and filled with God's life. In Presence, inner poverty counts as spiritual wealth and worldly wealth is often accounted as death to the spirit (cf. Mk. 10:23; Rom, 8:6).

Our lives are 'hidden with God' in Presence (cf. Col. 3:3). Our true identity is disclosed to us - and then only dimly - when we abide in Presence. Only God knows - and partially reveals - our real names when we enter the mystery of Presence (cf. Rev. 2:17).

Patience and Presence are synonymous. In Presence, we have nowhere to go and nowhere to be than where we are right here, right now. In Presence, we realize 'the kingdom of God has come upon us' (cf. Lk. 11:20). In Presence, we know that 'the kingdom of God is within us' (cf. Lk. 17:21).

Presence is the 'silver cord' that pulls us up and out of ourselves into God's heavenly realm (cf. Sir. 12:6–7). Presence is the divine updraft drawing us into the kingdom of God. In Presence, we resemble the deacon, Philip, who, 'caught up in the Spirit', was transported to another place (cf. Acts 8:39-40).

It is 'easier for a camel to pass through a needle' (cf. Lk. 18:25) than to thread our way through thinking into Presence. The 'gate is narrow and the way is hard that leads into Presence, and few are those who truly find it' (cf. Mt. 7:14; 22:14).

Presence is the 'thick cloud' and 'pillar of fire' that leads us out of the 'land of slavery' into the land of 'milk and honey' (cf. Ex. 13:2). Presence is our deliverer from distress and destruction (cf. Ex. 18:10; Jdg. 3:9; Ps. 107:20; Rom. 11:26). Presence is the divine Wisdom (Holy *Sophia*) who 'shelters us from the heat' and takes us 'into the midst of God's glory' (cf. Sir. 14:27).

Presence is contagious. Presence radiates like an electro-magnetic field. When we abide in Presence, others feel they could be healed 'if only they could touch the fringe of our garments' (cf. Mt. 14:36).

Knowing Presence is like knowing our guardian angel. Inseparable from us at all times and in all places, Presence rescues us from the dangers of impulsiveness, and pulls us back into the light when we are lost in the darkness. 'In distress', Presence 'calls to us' (cf. Ps. 81:7) and 'saves us from our calamities' (cf. 1 Sam. 10:19).

Presence is the true Mount of beatitude. In Presence, we realize how 'blessed we are' to be 'poor in spirit'. In Presence, 'the kingdom of heaven is ours'. In Presence, we are 'comforted when mourning'. In Presence, we are 'filled with a hunger and thirst for doing what is right'. In Presence, we even receive the inspiration to 'love our enemies and pray for those who criticize or condemn us' (cf. Mt. 5:3-12).

Presence is the heart of our identity in God, pumping divine lifeblood into us for the transfiguration of our bodies, minds, souls and spirits. Presence is the 'heart of flesh' that dissolves our 'hearts of stone' (cf. Ezek. 11:9; 36:26). In Presence, our hearts are tablets of the new commandment (cf. 2 Cor. 3:3) on which 'the finger of God' (cf. Lk. 11:20) inscribes the words of his Spirit (cf. 2 Cor. 3:3).

Holiness means dwelling in a continual state of Presence. Resting in Presence, we enter an 'eternal sabbath' (cf. Heb. 4:9). In Presence, we 'abide in a peaceful habitation, in secure dwellings, in God's quiet resting place' (cf. Isa. 32:18).

Sanctity means being saturated with Presence. In Presence, we are enriched and inebriated with God's own divinity. In Presence, we become 'new wine' that the 'old wineskins' of routine religion cannot hold (cf. Mk. 2:22).

Presence is at once a gift and a task, something we fundamentally are and something we need to acquire. The *desire* to be more present is itself Presence 'coming like a thief in the night' to awaken us to a more beatific way of living (cf. Mt. 24:43).

Presence hushes the kerfuffle. Presence silences our dramatics and quiets our histrionics. Presence exorcises our outbursts. In Presence, we become 'instruments of God's peace, sowing love where there is hatred, pardon where there is injury, faith where there is doubt, hope where there is despair and sadness where there is joy'.[77]

True authority, unassuming yet commanding, arises automatically in Presence. In Presence, we become one with the 'great high priest', not 'taking this honor upon ourselves, but called to it by God'. In Presence, we hear the words, 'You are my child, this day I have begotten you' (cf. Heb. 5:4–6).

Presence is infinitely gentle, even when it commands attention and imparts authority. In Presence, 'the bruised reed we break not, the smoldering wick we quench not' (cf. Isa. 42:3; Mt. 12:20).

Presence is an inner light leading us through the world's darkness. Presence gives us hope in 'the valley of death' (cf. Ps. 23:4) and joy amidst the 'daily troubles' of life (cf. Mt. 6:34). Presence is the light of God that no bushel basket can hide (cf. Mk. 4:21).

Presence allows us to remain self-possessed even when afraid or alarmed. Presence gives us calm amidst the wind and waves of our stormy world. In times of trouble, we can awaken Presence and hear the words, 'Be still!' (cf. Mk. 4:39).

---

[77] The song and poem of St. Francis of Assisi, *Make Me an Instrument of Your Peace*.

Presence is an inextinguishable source of hope and joy. No matter what happens, no matter what we have done or what the consequences of our actions, the moment all is placed in Presence, all is forgiven, all is redeemed. In Presence, 'all flesh can see the salvation of God' (cf. Lk. 3:6). In Presence, 'the grace of God has appeared for the salvation of all' (cf. Ti. 2:11).

Acknowledgement of our mistakes is already to have risen above them. The good we desire to do we cannot always do; the evil we wish to avoid we often do not do (cf. Rom. 7:16-19). In Presence, we are delivered from this dilemma. Presence is the risen Christ, saying to those who have abandoned him, 'Peace be with you' (cf. Lk. 24:36).

Presence is the fundamental structure of our existence, as well as an achievement of our agency as free creatures made in 'the image and likeness' of God (cf. Gen. 1:126-27). Similarly, Resurrection is a fundamental structure (*Logos*) of the cosmos, as well as an action of the One who himself is 'the Resurrection and the Life' (cf. Jn. 11:25). In Presence, we are one with Christ, the *Logos* of God, both in being and in action (cf. Jn. 17:22).

Practicing Presence, we need only to walk around to beautify the world and give hope to the hopeless. No amount of altruistic social work does as much good as a stroll in the park when practicing Presence. In Presence, we are one with Christ who, anointed with the Holy Spirit, 'went about doing good and healing all that were oppressed' (cf. Acts 10:38).

Presence is a power greater than ourselves in which we discover our true selves. In Presence, we awaken to an identity beyond what others may think of us, or even of what we think of ourselves. In Presence, we discover our union with God as the 'I am' of the 'I am this' or 'I am that'. In Presence, we discover ourselves as God knows us 'before we were conceived in our mothers' womb' (cf. Jer. 1:5; Lk. 2:21).

In Presence, we realize that all we have said or done apart from Presence is, in some sense, fraudulent. In Presence, like the disciples encountering the risen Christ whom they had abandoned and betrayed, we are utterly bewildered by what we are seeing (cf. Lk. 24:37-38). Discovering Presence, like encountering the risen Jesus, whether for the first time or again and again, is always an experience of disorienting, redeeming joy.

Presence is purgatory and heaven wrapped up as one. Presence dissolves our past evils in the blinding light of God's merciful judgment (cf. Acts 22:11). The uncreated light of God's immediate Presence is both purifying and redemptive. In Presence, like St. Paul, we are knocked from our high horses, at once blinded and illumined by God's unexpected grace (cf. Acts 22:7; Eph. 2:5).

Entering Presence is like having a Near Death Experience (NDE). In Presence, we momentarily die to the dynamics of this world, and enter the 'light in which there is no darkness' (cf. 1 Jn. 1:5). Returning to the workaday world after having been taken up into the Light, we desire that Presence become our only *modus operandi*, showing others the ultimate meaning of life.

The experience of Presence banishes remorse about the past and worries about the future. In Presence, we apprehend a light-filled *Plērōma* (fullness) 'which no eye can see and no ear can hear' (cf. 1 Cor. 2:9). In Presence, 'we are discharged from that which held us captive, so that we might live in the new life of the Spirit' (cf. Rom. 7:6).

Presence gives us a newfound and humble sense of our own limitations. In Presence, like Christ, we deem it a joy to 'consider equality with God nothing to be grasped at' (cf. Phil 2:6). Instead, we learn to 'swerve neither to the right nor to the left but to move instinctively away from evil' (cf. Prv. 4:27). In Presence, we learn 'to judge not, lest we be judged' (cf. Mt. 7:1; 1 Cor. 11:31).

In Presence, we learn how to stay in our own lane. In Presence, our 'eyes are not raised too high, nor do we occupy ourselves with things too great and too marvelous for us' (cf. Ps. 131:1). Instead, we resemble the Publican whose only prayer was, 'Lord, be merciful to me, a sinner' (cf. Lk. 18:13).

In Presence, we share in the virginal spirit of Mary whose 'soul proclaims the greatness of the Lord who has looked with infinite favor on his lowly servant' (cf. Lk. 1:48).

In Presence, we lose our need to perform, pretend, or posture. In Presence, God alone is the source of 'our strength and our salvation' (cf. Isa. 12:2). In Presence, we never 'rely on our own understanding' (cf. Prv. 3:5). In Presence, we know that 'all wisdom comes from the Lord and is with him for ever' (cf. Sir. 1:1).

In Presence, we discover our true strengths and weaknesses, preferences and aversions. In Presence, we embrace the whole of ourselves without shame or guilt, pride or apology. In Presence, we can enter 'the place of shame without resentment'.[78] In Presence, we are one with Christ who, when abandoned and betrayed, is 'never alone because the Father is with him' (cf. Jn. 16:32).

Presence is a place of perfect contentment, a place where we delight as much in our deficiencies as in our abilities. In Presence, we even 'boast of our weaknesses' (cf. 2 Cor. 12:9) since, in so doing, we resemble him who, 'though he was rich, yet for our sake he became poor, so that by his poverty we might become rich' (cf. 2 Cor. 8:9).

Presence is always an experience of amazing grace. When we've abided Presence for ten thousand years it will be as if we have just begun.[79]

---

[78] A seminal theme in the writings of James Alison. See: https://jamesalison.com/faith-beyond-resentment-introduction.

[79] Lyric from the hymn, *Amazing Grace.*